Decluttering &
Organizing SweetHome

The Best Advice to Decluttering and Cleaning
your Home, The Simple Tips for Useful
Decoration room by room, Creative Way for an
Orgnized Life.

BY

CELLINA EDGAR

i

Table of Contents

Signs You Have an Out of Control Home (OOCH)

It happens without warning. One day you notice your home has turned into a collage of papers, junk, and stuff - everywhere. You're not alone. Today more than ever it seems that the flotsam and jetsam of living, like the waves of an ocean, continually beat at our doors, flooding our houses with all manner of stuff until our homes are bulging at the seams. A typical home is now cluttered and dirty to the point of exhaustion -- yours.

All this accumulation also makes going home, or being at home, fill us with a sense of dread because we're overwhelmed by the sheer volume of things surrounding us. Once islands in the stream, many homes are often now just as jumbled, crowded, dirty, and chaotic as the public places we try to escape from. Housekeeping and cleaning house is not the greatest of fun, but it is vital to our well-being.

Recently a study by the UCLA Center for Everyday Lives of Families found that families are overscheduled, child-dominated, and cluttered. The study touched on something that's become a common problem in most households today: too much stuff. And all that stuff, makes us feel out of control.

Could your Home be Out of Control?

If you have a perfectly ordered home or just don't care about the state of your surroundings, then having an out of control home isn't a problem. But, if the thought of your home raises your blood pressure to an unhealthy level or spending time there would make you rather have your teeth drilled, then you do have a problem - and you may have a home that's out of control.

An out of control home is a source of frustration, embarrassment, and tension. So where do you start if this describes your home? The first step in learning how to cope with an out of control home is to recognize the signs. Only then can you address the problem.

1. It's Messy

Anything that can be straightened up in five minutes or less does not qualify as messy. A truly messy house has been hit by more than its fair share of bombs: toy bombs, clothes bombs, paper bombs (magazines, mail, and other piles of paper), dirt bombs (general dirt and debris), pet bombs (hair, smell, food), collectible or hobby bombs, etc. And, the mess is everywhere: the kitchen, the bathroom, the living room, the bedroom.

2. It's Disorganized

No one can find anything, from the car keys to last year's tax returns. A disorganized home is one where too much time is spent looking for things, and where you have doubles or triples of everything because when you couldn't find what you were looking for, you went out and bought another to replace the one you couldn't find.

3. It Stinks

The smell can come from the puppy training on the new carpet, the moldy smell from the roof leak, the cat box that's never changed, or the trash that everyone forgets to take out.

4. It's Dirty

This is that garden-variety filth that makes you hope no one will ever come to visit. It's the ring in the toilet, the dust bunnies the size of Dallas, and the cobwebs hanging from the ceiling that wave gently in the breeze. The dirt is pervasive and ground in.

5. It Doesn't Work

This is a home where the furniture is broken, the bed sags in the middle, things don't work like they should, and repairs that need to be made drag on for months or years. It's not truly functional and lots of things have "work-arounds," such as pliers to turn on the washing machine because the knob fell off.

6. It's Anxiety-Producing

Does the thought of going home make you feel anxious? If you're happier at work or in places other than home, then chances are it's because your home is out of control. It makes you uptight because it's dirty, disorganized, or messy - or all three. And, when you're there, you can't relax and you often find excuses to go somewhere else to unwind, such as at the movies or driving in the country.

7. You Avoid Having Visitors

If you feel panicked when the doorbell rings then you're living in an out of control home. Guests should be a welcome sight in the house and you should feel confident enough to invite visitors in.

8. It's Cluttered

If every square inch of your home is covered with something, then you've got too much stuff. There's got to be some open space somewhere in your home because open space give us a "visual rest." Look at interior design magazines and you'll notice the homes pictured in them because there isn't stuff everywhere to distract you.

Most Houses Have Out of Control Areas

Of course not all homes are out of control, but many homes suffer from one or more Out-Of-Control-Home (OOCH) symptoms, or they have an Out of Control Area (OOCA). These are areas such as the laundry room or garage that tends to get out of control, and most every home has one. But, regardless of whether your home is truly OOCH or OOCA, it doesn't have to stay that way. You can take steps to bring your house back to order and get it under control.

Use a "Declutter" List to Create Abundance in Your Life

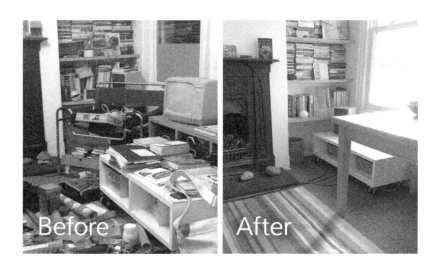

If you're anything like me, you recognize the need to declutter your home but you lack the motivation to do it. All of that junk, all the items that you've collected through the years, the dust, the dirt and the hours involved- the thought that you have to start to declutter your home is enough to drive you crazy!

Declutter for Convenience

A decision to declutter offers one clear advantage- there is a massive convenience factor! How many times have you been looking for a specific item, yet you're been unable to find it quickly and effectively. This is incredibly frustrating and even embarrassing, but you do not need to subject yourself to the stress of losing important documents and items in the mess within your home.

A decision to declutter is a decision to reorganize the documents and items that are important in your life and enable you to access them quickly and effectively when you need them. Downloading a guide from the Internet can help you in your quest to organize your home, and it is worth taking the time and expense to organize and set up your home effectively. A small amount of outlay can lead to a huge amount of convenience and lifestyle when you make the decision to declutter effectively.

Declutter for Appearances

A decision to declutter can dramatically improve the appearance of your home. Most visitors do not like to visit a chaotic or cluttered house, because it stresses them and makes them feel uncomfortable. It also can leave you feeling embarrassed at the state of your house when they visit, and this is a great motivation to help you decide to declutter probably.

Declutter for Your Family's Health

A decision to declutter can also improve your family's health. A messy and cluttered home is not only unsightly, but it is also a haven for dust, dirt, insects and even infestations. If you or anyone in your family suffers from atopic conditions such as eczema or asthma, the decision to declutter your home will not only make your home more livable but will lead to a direct increase in your family's health and well-being.

Save Serious Money

Do you shop to forget about your problems? If shopping makes you feel better about living, you may find your home too full of clutter fast.

Then there's the lost or misplaced items that you are constantly repurchasing and/or duplicating. When you get through the cleaning process, don't be surprised to find multiple rolls of tape, keys, money, shoes, tools, pens and a hundred other lost items.

Tip: As you toss duplicate and other needless items into your declutter, organize and clean hopper, make a list of the serious money you'll be saving in the future.

Increase Productivity

Want to gain a year in your life? NAPO reports the average American spends this much time looking for lost objects in his or her life!

Do you work from an office in your house? When you regularly have to struggle to find things such as scattered pens or even buried credit cards, for example, or search through or rearrange piles of paper, the process not only wastes time, but diverts your focus from your prime task and can eventually make you feel you're not fully professional.

Don't have a home office? Imagine, for example, how much easier a day of doing laundry is when organizing your soaps and cleaning supplies means you can locate things immediately. Multiply that by other areas, such as your kitchen pantry, garage or the dreaded bedroom closet, and you can see what rich by-products decluttering brings.

Elevate Self Esteem

Do you want an instant self-esteem boost? Then declutter, organize and simplify where you live! You'll feel better about yourself as it all comes together. A sense of accomplishment, relief, and joy almost always follows. You'll also be more able to relax in your surroundings when you are not tripping over toys, shoes and other common clutter.

Start to Declutter Now

It is very true that the decision to declutter your home can be a scary, indeed terrifying decision to have to make. However, when you stand back and look at the end results of your decision, you will recognize the benefits of making the right decision far outweigh the difficulty, cost and hours you put in to cleaning, organizing and decluttering your home.

A chaotic and messy home is not only unsightly, it is also unhealthy, stressful and extremely frustrating. In fact, if you want a new lease of life, a change in the appearance of your home, the well-being of your family and the general audience of your home, they're one of the best decisions you can ever make is to not delay but decide to declutter your home now.

Maintain an Efficient, Orderly Entryway

A front entry should be an area that invites you in and provides comfort from the outside world, but if it's overrun with coats, boots and shoes, pet leashes, mail and backpacks, it's will seem more chaotic than comforting. If you want to redecorate your foyer to make it more visually appealing, the first thing you need to do is control clutter.

First, Evaluate and Relegate

Before you think about colors and beautiful accessories, think about how you and your family use your foyer. First consider whether you even need to use it everyday as you come and go. Would the back entry or an entry off the garage into a mud room or laundry make life a little easier by containing the mess before it enters the house? If so, you may want to change your family's habit of using the front door. We'll talk a little later about how to control clutter at the back entry.

If your family really must use your front entrance everyday, then you need to add storage that makes the space more functional. If you have a closet in or near the entry, empty it and reorganize it so that it can better accommodate all the coats and outdoor gear that is constantly coming and going. If there is no closet with convenient access, a bench with storage above and below can help get things organized. Some come with cubbies that offer storage for everything from hats to book bags. Decorative wall hooks can provide a spot for jackets, bags, and leashes and a table in the entry can be used with lidded baskets for handy yet discreet storage. Choose a table with drawers for even more storage space. A table also provides a convenient place to drop keys and mail each day.

If shoes must stay in the front entry, a boot tray can help keep muddy messes from traveling beyond the front hall.

Back Door Solutions

Back entries can become dumping grounds for garden and pet supplies as well as toys, sport gear and outdoor wear. Your first line of defense is to store items elsewhere when possible: You really don't need your garden tools at the ready in the middle of February, so can they go to the garage or tool shed until spring? Surfboards in December and snow skis in July add to the feeling of disorganization, so switch and store elsewhere whenever possible.

A good size boot tray and wall hooks or bench and storage system are essential for keeping coats, scarves, bags and pet leashes close at hand but still neat and tidy. Pet food and garden supplies can be stored in stackable bins and shoes can be tucked on shelves inside a closet. Seasonal items, such as garden hand tools, can be kept in a bucket so that you can pick them up and go whenever you're ready. Wall shelves are an excellent way to corral small items in metal, wood or wicker boxes or to make a display of utilitarian items, such as vases, doggie biscuit canisters, or your fishing tackle box.

Putting Paper in Its Place Using The P-L-A-N Technique

Do any of these problems ring true for you?

1. Are you collecting piles because you don't have a "home" for objects?

2. Are you missing time-sensitive deadlines, like due-dates on bills?

3. Are all the drawers full or do you need new categories for your filing?

4. You don't have any time or hate to file?

5. Need to do some archiving or storage of old taxes, etc?

6. Are you afraid to start for some reason? Does this have to do with procrastination or perfectionism?

Why is paper so pervasive, so daunting? Why do we have a national epidemic of paper? Consumerism puts the pressure on us to constantly buy-buy-buy. The Wall Street Journal states that the average business person wastes 6 weeks a year looking for things on his/her desk. That's over an hour a day and accounts for a loss of over $8 million in lost time!

- Sheer volume! The U S Postal Service sends out over 200 billion pieces of mail each year! If you aren't vigilant, you'll never get caught up. It grows and grows unless you sort and purge continually! A home office is more time-consuming than organizing a garage!

- Think before you print! Is it available elsewhere? Are you really going to read it later?

- Pareto Principle: 80/20: "I might need it someday", but are you aware that only 20% of what you file is ever accessed again?

- Clutter is unmade decisions, where objects have no "home", particularly paper! It doesn't enrich your life. Clutter costs time and money and can strain your various relationships. It makes it hard to maintain balance and can suck the life right out of you! Paper is NOT going away, as we heard years back. Be vigilant about keeping it out of your home and office as much as possible. It can own you if you don't deal with it regularly!

When you organize or throw items away, you gain the self-confidence and inner peace that completing a tough project affords, feel more prepared and focused and you have more time and money. You'll feel like you have your sanity back! Better yet, eliminate as much of your stuff as you can! The P-L-A-N © acronym can be used in almost any planning situation. Planning is at the forefront of accomplishing anything in an orderly, successful manner. Yes, what we're talking about is good old-fashioned time management! Let's get started!

P is for PREPARE:

Visualize: Where are your papers now? Counter? Desk? Kitchen or dining room table?

Close your eyes for a minute. Imagine your perfect home office, or bill-paying center or that all your photos are organized. What does that area look like? You know, you can't hit a target that you can't see, so you need to define what that target is! Good intentions or the desire to change are not sufficient without a vision, a plan. When you focus on your vision, you can turn that into reality. Make sure, however, that it is shared with others who will also be using the system, so they can follow it and its ideals. Base your vision on your values and what's important to you. This will give you a roadmap to create the plan, which will give you confidence and an increase of energy.

Plan, list, prioritize and schedule: These will be the GPS for your organizing project!

Identify and list your problem areas and make the decision to attack one of them. It can either be the one that is driving you the craziest or maybe a smaller one, just to get something done and give you that mental boost of confidence to carry on. It is also generally better to work on one small area at a time, rather than becoming overwhelmed by the entirety of a project. One of the tools you can use for planning a project is a Mind Map. This helps you focus, breaks a large job into smaller, easier to handle pieces and helps guide you where you want to go. In the center, write the project that you plan to work on first. As you use the Mind Map and complete one arm (or leg) on the map, start work on another, based upon the priorities you have determined.

Take inventory of the space available: what do you already have in the way of file cabinets, desk drawers, supply cabinets and bookcases? If the project you are going to work on is your photo collection, what do you already have in the way of albums or photo boxes? Inadequate or incomplete storage or inefficient furniture placement could also be the cause of your disorganization.

Define zones: where IS paper allowed? You need to designate a home for each type of paper and paper activity, such as art projects. It's not going away on its own!

Pick a date, put it on the calendar and keep this appointment with yourself! You now have an obligation of when you are going to start your project. Try to work for at least half an hour so you can see your accomplishment take form. If you think it will be too boring or tedious, have a friend to help make you accountable. Maybe you can even trade time to help each other, so you are both getting your paper under control!

Now, let's go to the next item, L is for LAUNCH INTO ACTION:

Now we are ready to talk about the actual work of clearing the mess! Be sure to focus, focus, focus! Don't pause to take actions at this point. No phone calls, no emails, no reading!

Storage systems and methodologies need to be simple! They also need to be functional for you, because each of us operates under different parameters of what works and doesn't work. Remember: there is no such thing as perfection. Aim for "good enough." What that is changes throughout your life. You can be organized one moment, go through a period of disorganization, back to feeling organized, etc., all dependent upon the degree and intensity of life changes and what strategies you have for regrouping and getting back "into the groove."

Proper containers, tools, labeling, ongoing evaluation and maintenance to"tweak" the system will make it appropriate for you! No matter which acronym you use, use that philosophy to get your organizing rolling. Examples are: *FAT(TM): File/Act/Toss; RAT: Retain/Act/Toss; START(TM): Sort/Throw/Appoint a home/Restrict to a container/Take back control.*

SORT and PURGE:

Have supplies available for sorting: empty boxes or banker boxes for temporary sorting, hanging and interior folders, recycle trash containers, shredder handy.

Do a "quick sort" initially. Generally, 2/3 of what you find can either be filed or trashed, with the remainder requiring some sort of follow-up. Jot the date in the corner of the papers you are going to keep, if they aren't already dated. This will make purging easier if/when you come across that document again.

As you sort each piece of paper (yes - each!), ask questions like these:

- Is this time-sensitive?
- Are there tax or legal considerations regarding this paper?
- Is this something I need to refer to regularly?
- Does this pertain to something major I am working on, such as a current project?
- Would my life change if I didn't save this piece of paper?
- Is it available elsewhere?

You will be making a decision on each item you encounter (photo, paper, magazine, etc): do I keep this? If so, where? Toss it? File it? Archive it? Don't try to sort every paper in every pile in your home at one time! Concentrate on the area you want organized first, then move into the other areas.

Toss all duplicates: mailings, ads, magazines - new one in/old one out! Toss junk mail, warranties and instructions for appliances and other items you no longer own.

Keep for up to seven years: financial and tax info, bank records, sales records of investments, CD's, tax return documentation. Retention guidelines vary by state, the IRS rules change over time and industry standards also change for certain employment situations. Be conservative: the IRS can audit up to six years' back taxes, but if they think fraud might be involved, there is no time limit. If you have monthly or quarterly financials, you can generally destroy them once you have received the yearly data. Information on your filed tax returns, 401K, IRA, home, vital records (such as birth and death certificates, passports, marriage certificates, power of attorney, medical records, Social Security, wills. etc.) should be kept permanently. Be sure to consult a lawyer or accountant for definitive information on specific "musts."

Keep data on the following for as long as you own the item: vehicles, insurance policies, investments, major appliance purchases.

ACT and STORE:

Where depends on the type of document: Its "home" might be a file, an archive box or a safe deposit box. Make sure you place "like" things together, where you can find and use them again.

You need to have a place, a home, for all incoming paper: an "in box." This should be for "active" papers only, things that require you to do something. If you don't need to do anything with it, then that paper either needs to be filed, go to a designated "to be filed" location or tossed (recycled or shredded).

You must have a work area, where you have a good working surface, file storage and access to your supplies. If you don't have a desk, you will need to set up a paper "command center" somewhere, generally where you will do the work. If you pay your bills at the kitchen table and your file cabinet is located in the rec room downstairs, you might get the papers down to the top of that cabinet, but not filed inside! In this situation, maybe a rolling cabinet that can be pulled out from a hall closet might work best for you. Metal is better than plastic, but you have to do what works with your reality, primarily the space you have and your budget,

The main purpose of a filing system is NOT storage, but retrieval! Filing cabinets or drawers don't have to be "black holes" where things go in, never to be found again! Maybe you don't have your system set up properly for you. You want an easy system that is efficient, where everything is close at hand, so you can just swivel, roll or reach your way to it. If you are not using what you currently have set up, there is something wrong with it and you need to fix it! Is it too complicated? Too boring? Inconvenient? Make the changes and make it fun! You can use color-coding (not too involved!); change tab positions for ease of use; label your categories for ease of retrieval (black on white is best).

There are many different filing systems out there. Make note if you are a "piler" or a "filer." You can't expect success if you are going "against the grain" of your natural tendencies. Keep in mind that it's hard to prioritize from a pile, though. You would first need to sort through that pile to at least rearrange it into various action categories, such as to read, to do, to file, etc. There are systems so involved that you will never use all the components supplied. There are systems so wonderfully simple that you don't try them because you think it needs to be more complex. Self-purging filing systems, or a personal obligation to make sure you purge regularly, is half the battle of keeping up with the paper!

You will generally want to group financial papers together, such as bills, pay stubs, bank statements, tax statements, etc. Personal information will also be grouped, such as medical/dental, home décor or hobbies, warranties, places to go, etc. Hanging files with broad categories, such as Medical/Dental, with files within for family members, different doctors, insurance claims, etc. are great. And you know what? There's nothing wrong with the old A-Z alphabet, either! Be sure to place the files used most often in the most accessible location.

Mail/Bills/Receipts/Tax Info:

These you want to get systemized right away, because not taking care of these on time costs you money in late fees, makes you lose the best interest rates and ruins your credit ratings.

If you can, pay bills via autopay or online. This keeps the clutter down, payments are credited almost instantly and it's "greener" - you have kept one more piece of paper on this planet from being generated!

Again, define the zone! Designate one container for all incoming mail, whether it's a file folder or a tray. As soon as it arrives, put it in this stated place - home! Make sure it's convenient, with all the supplies you will need kept handy. Set up a weekly, bi-monthly or monthly time to attend to bills, which is usually dependent on pay cycles.

Photos/Kids' Artwork:

If you do nothing else with photos already developed, label the envelopes with the date range and the events contained within. If you are still using film or developing prints, follow this practice as you bring new photos into the home. There a many wonderful online sites available now to help you create photo books or scan photos of your children's artwork to be saved for posterity, starting at about $15. Acid-free photo boxes are very attractive and functional; with tabbed dividers for labeling categories, special occasions, etc. which makes retrieval easy.

Photo albums are more expensive, cumbersome and don't allow for some of the creativity that the online albums do. However, they are wonderful for certain memories, such as weddings. I, personally, am giving myself this year to break the photo-album cycle and try something new!

Newpapers, Magazines, Catalogs, Other Reading Materials:

These are objects that can be dealt with at a slower pace, as time and energy allows. They are also easier to purge - new one in, old one out. In 2003, the U S Post Office delivered over 20 billion catalogs in the U.S. alone. That's enough for 70 catalogs for every man, woman and child in this country! Call the toll-free numbers on the back of catalogs to have your name removed from their mailing system.

When you do order something, make sure you note "Do not sell, rent, lease or trade my name" on the order form. Don't complete and return the registration cards when you purchase something. That just gets your information sold to any number of other companies!

Calendars/To-Do Lists/Time Management Planners:

The choices are overwhelming! PDAs can be expensive and time-consuming to learn all the bells and whistles and you are always fidgeting with them. They are the choice for many people, though. Paper calendars also have a good-and-bad side: wall calendars are great to see the whole family's activities at a glance, but that doesn't do you any good if you're away from home. Portable calendars are easy to take with you, but the boxes are usually very small. Determine what you need: how many time slots do you need to keep track of? Odds are, you won't need 15-minute increments for your home calendar, but you might at work.

There are some great online reminder/note/calendar systems out there right now, to use in conjunction with your laptop or PC. For on-the-go reminder-retrieval, "web-clipping", recipes, etc., take a look for such sites.

So, that brings us to "A" of the method: ADJUST AND ADAPT!

Realize that as times change, your abilities and circumstances change, so paper management systems have to change, too!! Otherwise, you are just adding to the chaos of whatever is going on at the time and you become even more overwhelmed.

Control what comes into your home! There is so much out there! Try to be selective and choose to read or deal with that which you enjoy the most. Carry some of that reading with you so when you get the chance and have a few minutes, you can read without stress or guilt! Cancel subscriptions that you don't have time to read. You'll save time, money, guilt and yet more clutter from entering your home! You could even subscribe to online newspapers.

Set up a routine maintenance plan to help establish new habits. When the mail comes, handle it all at a time that allows you to complete it, from making necessary phone calls to filing. Fine tune it and monitor it to stay in control. Nothing is perfect and this is a learning experience: what you like, don't like, what you are able to handle. Then, if a crisis arises, you will be under less stress and not so distracted, enabling you to handle it better. Sort out and purge constantly. If things creep back in that you just weeded out, you now know how to handle them! If you find that you are eventually ignoring your system, it's definitely time to revamp it.

"N" is for N-JOY!!

Relax/reward/repeat for the next project! Make it fun! Celebrate!

Now is the time to determine a project you want to attack, get it on the calendar and get set for planning that accomplishment! Trust me: you will find now that you have more confidence to get the job done, have more energy to do it, be happy doing it and revel in the peace of mind that completing each project gives you!

Keep on organizing - one step at a time. If you see a pile, deal with it! Watch out for flat surfaces - they have a tendency to collect anything and everything! If you're done with something, put it away! If you don't have any more room for certain items, it's time to begin the process of sorting and purging again!

In closing, my goal in this chapter was to introduce you to methods of dealing with the mass of paper that inundates our homes. We've talked about why it's here; how to attack and control it; how to store it or make it disappear! Through creating a vision and well-laid plans, you've learned the process for making all that happen and hopefully see now that you are the boss of that stuff! Remember that real change only happens when you take action, and this action will allow you to find the peace of mind and serenity that you want in your home.

Do you think that you can go home now and be successful in eliminating one of the piles or messes that are driving you crazy? I know you can! Happy Organizing!

Stop That Junk Mail – Please!

Y ou can simplify your life and even avoid information pornography, but if you're like most people, your email inbox is still bursting at the seams, your voicemail is full, and you're getting slammed with too much stuff.

To make matters worse, you get flooded with old-fashioned mail. It's a cause of real stress and anxiety. Why? In the wise words of Newman from Seinfeld: "Because the mail never stops. It just keeps coming and coming and coming, there's never a let-up. It's relentless. Every day it piles up more and more and more!"

To avoid going Newman, er, I mean postal, you need an effective system to capture and process your mail quickly. The key to any system is to make sure it works when life is calm but also when you are crazed and have a hundred things going on at once.

If you follow these four steps, you will be able to control your mail once and for all. It might seem like a lot of work initially, but once you set this up, it will run smoothly and effortlessly.

Step 1 – Dump

You'll need one big bin labeled "Unsorted Inbox." Whenever you get the mail, you can dump it all into this bin, or if you have some time, you can skip directly to the "Sorting" step below.

Step 2 – Sort

If there are multiple people in your house that receive mail, you will still need an Unsorted Inbox bin, but you'll also need a separate inbox tray for each person. For example, if you're married and have two high school children, you would need one inbox bin and four trays-one for each family member. Each of the trays should be marked with a family member's name (e.g., Robert's Inbox, Mary's Inbox).

If Junior grabs the mail as he's heading out to football practice, he can throw everything into the Unsorted Inbox. Then when mom comes home and has a few extra minutes, she can take everything out of the Unsorted Inbox and sort it (i.e., go through each piece of mail and dispense it to the correct inbox.

Step 3 – Screen

Screening is the process of going through your inbox and separating the important mail from the not-so-important and putting it into the following three trays/folders/baskets:

- Magazines/Catalogs

- "Junk" Mail to Shred (junk mail that doesn't need to be shredded can be tossed immediately during this step)

- Everything Else

If there are multiple people at your house, ideally each person would not only have their own inbox but they would also have their own three screening trays. I like the idea of making the inboxes portable so you can pick up your inbox and take it with you to the den, bedroom, office, etc. and Screen/Process on your own turf. Plus, you won't have 100 bins/trays clogging up your kitchen.

Step 4 – Process

Once your mail has been screened, you then need to process it. Processing your mail involves opening it and determining what the next action is:

Magazines/Catalogs – No rush to do anything here. You can let these pile up, and then when you have down time, you can go through them. If you're heading to the doctor, dentist, or getting your oil changed, grab a handful of magazines/catalogs to take with you while you wait.

"Junk" Mail to Shred – The action here is to shred this stuff. Keep a shredder nearby so you can quickly and easily get rid of this mail.

Everything Else – This is the meat of your mail. When you go through the Everything Else tray, you'll probably throw some things away that may have looked important but was actually junk mail. But for most of the contents in the Everything Else tray, there will be some action to take such as pay a bill, read a letter, review a bank statement, etc.

You can either do whatever action is required right then, or you can put mail with like actions in the same folder. For example, you can create a "Pay Bills" folder and put all of your bills in it. Twice a month you can grab all the bills from this folder and pay them. Or you can have a "Statements Review" folder where you would put all of your bank and investment account statements you want to review at some later point.

The number of action folders is really up to you. Start with a few basics such as "Pay Bills" and "Statements Review." If you discover there is another recurring action, you can then create a folder for it.

You can't stop the mail (just ask Kramer), but you can certainly manage it. But what about all of the other documents and information in your life? I'm glad you asked. I'm working on a series that will help you take back control of your life and all the stuff in it. Because when you aren't drowning in information and mail, you can spend more of your other 8 hours writing books, becoming a better public speaker, investing in yourself, learning, and creating.

Organize Your Bedroom For the Best Sleep of Your Life

When you have trouble sleeping, do you reach for sleep aids to cure your insomnia? You are not alone. But the consequences of chronic sleep aid use can be devastating to your health. Not only can sleep aids cause depression, new research has shown that some sleep aid users can develop an eating disorder from taking sleeping pills!

"One woman gained 100 pounds before finally realizing that Ambien was at fault...Sleep-eating can occur spontaneously or in association with other drugs, so Ambien may not be the only culprit. But the researchers think that there's something about Ambien that leads to sleep-eating in some people. Presumably only a very small percentage of users are susceptible, but with millions of Americans taking Ambien every year, the sleep-eaters could number in the thousands."Source: New York Times Editorial, March 14, 2006

It's amazing the ripple effects a single behavior can have on the rest of your life. It's like that with organizing, too. Once you start rearranging your time, space and stuff, the ripple effects can lead to remarkable improvements in your overall energy, happiness, and even your health! The process of organizing requires that you make some tough decisions and become clear about your values and purpose.

The very act of taking charge of your stuff to make it work to support your true intentions is empowering. This is especially true in bedrooms. Many people view the bedroom as a place to put everything they don't want other people to see, or as a multifunctional space. They watch TV, exercise, work and more in the bedroom. The ripple effect of this is often insomnia, stress and related health problems. Getting clear about the purpose of your bedroom, and organizing it to support your intention will have dramatic effects on how well you sleep.

I was a chronic insomniac who took melatonin every night to help me sleep. Using a combination of organizing principles and Feng Shui strategies, I kicked the sleep aid habit and now get the best sleep of my life! Here are my top tips to help you get the sleep you need to stay energized, happy and healthy.

1. Take Things That Don't Support Sleep and Romance Out of Your Bedroom

The purpose of your bedroom is ultimately to support you in distressing and recharging you to be ready to deal with life. It should serve you by helping you relax and sleep well. If you aren't sleeping well, take a good look around your room. Do you have a computer or work desk in there? Exercise equipment? TV? Telephone? And if you have them all in there, it's no wonder you have trouble sleeping! They don't do anything to help you relax or get to sleep. Find new homes for them. Taking telephone out of our bedroom made a big difference for me. If you need to have one in your bedroom, at least turn the ringer off. Sleep is too important to let wrong numbers or telemarketers wake you up!

2. Clear the Clutter!

If your bedroom is full of clutter, your mind will be cluttered too. If your mind is cluttered, it's impossible to relax and sleep. Without a clutter-free foundation, the tips below won't be as effective. So start with the floor and the surfaces in your room. Later, go deeper into closets and drawers. Clear out the things you no longer use and donate them to someone who can use them. Put things in their proper home. If they don't have a home, make one for them. Throw out or repair anything that is broken. Finish things that are undone or get rid of them. Put your laundry in the hamper. Better yet, take the laundry out of the room and clean it! Clutter is stagnant energy. Clearing clutter is the foundation to releasing stuck energy and getting a good night's sleep.

3. Give everything in Your Room a Home so You can KEEP it Free of Clutter

One of the most common sources of clutter in the bedroom is clothing you've worn, but it's not dirty, so you don't want to put in the hamper yet. Designate a space for your "gently worn" clothing. This can be hooks placed on a door or inside your closet; a special drawer; a wardrobe shelf; a coat rack, or even a chair -- just keep them neat and don't use the floor or your bed! To maintain a clutter-free room, things need a home where it will be easy for you to find them again, AND where it will be easy to put them away. If you have drawers, but never put things in them, get rid of them. Use shelves or a wardrobe instead. If you don't have one, get a table or nightstand with a drawer or a private decorative box to keep near your bedside. Keep all your incidentals contained -- like earplugs, lotions, tissues, lint brushes, scissors, etc. so they don't contribute to clutter. If you have a lot of junk on your dresser, sort like with like, and put it away in one of the drawers. Use drawer dividers to give each thing a home. Designate a drawer or shelf for purses. Be creative. You don't have to do the things the way everyone else does. The only rule is that things need a home so they don't become clutter.

4. Dust!

Keep your bedroom as well dusted as you can. Excess dust in your room makes it harder for you to breathe. It can cause allergy symptoms and seriously disturb your sleep. Keep dusting wipes in a utility room near your bedroom so that you can easily dust frequently. Especially if you have pets. Remember, don't only do the surfaces! Many people let dust collect under beds, furniture, on curtains, etc. for months and sometimes even years. Do in-depth dusting 2-4 times a year and you will sleep much better.

5. Position your Bed Advantageously

In the practice of Feng Shui, placement of objects is essential to encouraging positive energy flow. You should be able to see the door from your bed, but not have your bed directly in front of the door. A power position in the room allows you to feel more secure and sleep better overall.

6. Change the Sheets!

Your sheets can be a source of your insomnia in part because they collect dust. But they also absorb your energy! Sounds a little weird I know, but it's true. Think about it. You spend 6-8 hours a night in them. And, don't you usually sleep best when you have nice clean fresh sheets? If you don't believe me, try it anyway! What could it hurt? Make sure you change your sheets at least once a week, but for some people who are very sensitive to energy and dust, every 3 to 5 days works much better. If you have trouble sleeping, color could be part of the problem. Sheets in soft, restful colors like white, soft green and blue are the most relaxing.

7. Do a Comfort and Ergonomics Check

Are your pillows the right ones for you? Is your bed soft enough to not cut off your circulation during the night? Are the colors in your room soothing? Does your alarm clock wake you up gently or do you hate the sound of it? I found it much easier to wake up once I started using a "dawn-simulating" alarm clock.

8. Let the Light and Air in

Refresh the energy in your room daily. Open your blinds and let the natural light in. If you can, air the room for at least 15 minutes as well. Fresh air is a great way to help you sleep better. Don't you always find you sleep great after a day outdoors?

Bonus tips:

9. Watch What You Eat

Are you snacking on chocolate, soda, or other foods that may have hidden caffeine in them after dinner? Are you eating sugary foods or foods with lots of chemicals in them before bed? What you eat, and when you eat it can seriously affect your sleep. If you snack before bed, choose whole, unprocessed foods as much possible! Nuts, fruit, raw veggies, and homemade low salt popcorn are far better choices than candy, chocolate, ice cream or other dessert foods. Plan ahead to avoid snacking on junk foods before bed.

10. Use Earplugs

If you have a partner that snores, or even if you yourself snore, stop waking yourself up! Using earplugs changed my life and saved my marriage. Not only do I snore, so does my husband! We both used to wake ourselves and each other up constantly. Now, we both sleep much more restfully. It takes a little getting used to, but the rewards are well worth it. I can even sleep in hotels now! I recommend the soft foam type of earplugs. If they are too big, you can trim them to size.

12. Keep a Pen and Paper by Your Bedside

If you can't sleep, often it's because your mind is racing. Perhaps you are getting lots of ideas to solve a problem at work, or you are worried about a meeting tomorrow. Whatever is rolling around in your brain and won't stop, you need to get your thoughts on paper so you can get them off your mind! This helps clear your mental clutter so you can rest!

These tips will get you well on your way to organizing your life so you can get a good night's sleep! If you can't do them all alone or aren't sure which are right for you, get help. Your sleep is too important. It affects your physical, mental, and even spiritual health. It's not worth risking your health with the chronic use of sleep aids.

Sweet Dreams!

Pantry Check – Do You Know What's in There?

It is my belief that every home needs a well-organized pantry. If you don't have the luxury of a walk in pantry, don't despair! You should be able to designate and organize an area in your home to serve as the pantry. Even if you put up shelves in your basement.

The benefits of maintaining a well-stocked and neatly organized pantry are numerous. A bonus is that you won't have to make as many trips to the store. If you follow these easy steps that I have outlined in this article for you -- by starting with keeping items inventoried and making a complete list of what you need to purchase -- it will not only save you much aggravation, but will allow you to use the coupons you have clipped and purchase items on sale and even in bulk, saving you: gas, time and money! As well as your sanity!

Function – First in the Pantry

It does not matter how large or small your pantry is, but FUNCTION needs to be your first consideration. Here are a few functional tips for organizing your pantry:

- Just like organizing any room in your home, a pantry should be planned to save time, energy, efficiency; and therefore, money!
- Your pantry should be well-lit so that you can see all areas.
- Make your pantry efficient for you. It should be located centrally in your home. Either in the kitchen or a hall closet that is relatively close to your work area. If needed, it is perfectly fine to create multiple pantry

areas. If doing this, just remember to organize each space so that the items needed in the kitchen are in the kitchen, cleaning supplies separate from food, and bedding and bath linens are near your home's bedrooms and bathrooms, and so on.

- Consider the humidity and temperature of your pantry; you don't want to store dry food items in a damp place and a pantry that has a relatively cool, constant temperature is ideal.

- If space is limited, buy plastic storage containers that you can stack in a coat closet, on top of closet shelves, and/or even under your bed. In these containers, I would keep items that you access less often in these storage areas. If you buy in bulk to save money and keep the excess inventory in these less easily accessed areas, you can always restock a smaller supply in your most convenient pantry storage area.

- Keeping a "good inventory" of the items you use regularly will allow you to be able to avoid tempting sale prices on items you don't use and/or you don't need.

Getting Started – Cleaning Out The Pantry

Now that you have planned your pantry for function, it is now time to get started on reorganizing!

Once you have established your pantry area, you'll want to start by removing everything - I know, I know - don't freak - by removing everything will be able to help you get started and in order.

1. Empty your pantry completely - moving everything into boxes, tabletops and/or counter tops. Discard or recycle anything that you find is spoiled, expired, stale or otherwise unusable.

2. Before setting about to put things in order - you are going to have fun by disassembling whatever food cupboards you currently use. Look at everything as you take it out and consider the following: How long has it been since you used that item? For example, Herbs - loose a great deal of flavor after 6 months even in a dark, cool space. While you're at it check expiration date and throw away accordingly. Remember the rule: When in doubt, Throw it out!

3. Clean any dust or dirt off of each item as you go.

4. If something has lost it's label, but you know for certain what it is, make either a handmade (or digital created) label for easy recognition and mount it to your container.

5. The best part about this process - even if it is time consuming, is that it only has to be done twice a year. Plan to do it in the Spring and Fall.

6. Clean the shelving and walls thoroughly with a solution of warm water and mild soap, drying them with a towel and by letting the shelf surfaces dry thoroughly.

Preparation – Pantry Space

Once you have removed everything, cleaned and prepared your pantry space, you are ready to start re-organization. This is the fun part!

Here are my suggested steps for getting your pantry ready for increased efficiency, order and money saving!

1. As you begin to organize your "Well-Stocked Pantry"...look for any available space you can use to store items; the back of a pantry door can be used to store spices and other small items if you hang a rack over the door. You can purchase these racks at either: Bed Bath and Beyond, Home Depot, Lowes, Target and or any other similar retail store.
2. If needed, now is the time to repaint your pantry walls and shelves. I believe that white or off-white is generally the best color for a pantry. It shows cleanliness!
3. At this point, you can lay down some easily wipe-off surface paper on your shelves. This will protect your shelf surfaces from stains.

4. Your next step is organizing your shelves according to the contents that you want to keep in your "Well-Stocked Pantry."

5. I suggest getting some of Tupperware's Modular Mate containers. They are great for keeping dry goods such as flour, sugar, pasta, teabags, coffee beans, and cereal. I believe that using rectangular or square containers will take up less space and stack more neatly than round or oval shaped containers.

The Pantry Re-Organizing

Now that you have cleaned out your pantry, you can begin to get things organized by using the following steps:

1. Start by sorting pantry items into categories: Examples include: fruits, vegetables, soups, condiments, boxed lunches/dinners, canned meats, sauces, baking goods, and rice/pasta/dry beans. While you're doing this first round of categorizing, be sure to put the items in order by their expiration dates, by putting the soonest expiring being the last item to go back into the pantry (i.e. it will be in front, thereby reducing wastefulness).

2. The heaviest of items should go on the lower shelves. Especially if you have a lazy Susan installed. For example, you have a large can of Tomato Sauce, put it on the lowest shelf with the canisters for your baking goods. In the meantime, leave the upper shelves open for those items

that you use frequently, and lighter weight items like beans, pasta and/or rice.

3. By using canisters you can keep dry goods and baking items such as: flour and sugar, fresh and bug free. You can keep smaller items, such as tea and coffee, dried fruits and bouillon in small baskets and/or plastic bins, which also helps keep them fresh.

4. Group items that are alike together: breakfast items, snack items, baking goods, cleaning supplies, dish linens, etc. It is important that if you take a bit of time to consider how things are arranged in the grocery store where you typically shop, you can group your pantry items similarly. Using subgroups will help to keep things more neatly stored and easily accessible. For example, all canned goods go on one shelf, organized into subgroups such as: fruits, vegetables, soups, crackers and cookies, etc.

5. Labeling shelves will help you keep your groups in order.

Pantry Inventory List and Restocking

Now that you have cleaned your "Well-Stocked Pantry," have discarded outdated items, added shelving (if needed), you will want to take inventory. By doing this it will help you to determine what is missing and what needs to be regularly re-supplied.

For your convenience, I have created a starter list of common items you may want to keep in your pantry and add to your own pantry inventory list:

* Canned Items - Soup, Broths, Vegetables, Fruit, Beans, Tomatoes, etc.; * Jar Foods - Tomato Paste and Sauce, Olives, Pickles, Peanut Butter, Jams and Jellies * Baking Items - Baking Powder, Baking Soda, Flour, Sugar, Extracts and more! * Spices - Salt, Pepper, Basil, Italian Season, Tarragon, Paprika, Crushed Red Pepper and more! * Starches - Pasta, Potatoes, Rice * Condiments - Soy Sauce, Vinegar, Ketchup, Mustard, Mayonnaise * Sweeteners - Syrup, Honey, Artificial Sweetener * Dry Goods - Cereals, Oatmeal, Pancake Mix, Raisins & Dried Fruit, Nuts & Seeds * Oils - Olive Oil, Canola Oil, Peanut Oil, Vegetable Oil, etc.

Keeping The Pantry Well Organized

Now that you have your pantry cleaned and organized, you will want to follow these few easy tips to keep it that way:

1. Don't buy things that won't get used; this will save money!
2. Do buy only according your tastes, budget and needs.
3. Look for coupons and sale items to keep in your pantry

4. Use your pantry regularly, checking your inventory to be sure that you are not overstocked.

5. If possible, items such as paper towels, paper plates, napkins, etc. that will not expire or become stale, purchase in larger quantities.

The Wrap-Up

If possible, try to buy reserve quantities of the staple items that you use the most. This will avoid "out-of-stock" items. Having an extra jar of mayo or some reserve cans of chicken and/or tuna salad can come in very handy with a surprise visit from a friend. Be sure to add these items to your shopping list when you break into your reserves. With kids in the house, you might want to consider making a special area and/or basket where you can keep quick snacks and treats handy. This will help keep the kids out the pantry! Homemade trail mix is a great snack and easy to store!

I have found that it is best to try to reorganize your pantry when you are alone, or have a block of time available for you to concentrate and complete the project quickly!

Remember to store cleaning products and chemicals away from your food items!

Keep items that you use the most often in front and readily visible!

Stack cans, jars and other items so that the labels can be easily read.

Always be on the lookout for new organization aids such as: baskets, wire baskets, adjustable racks, stacking containers, and more that will improve your pantry organization.

Make a "guest" or "refreshment" shelf to keep crackers, dips, chips, drink mixes and other items handy so you are ready to have an impromptu party or your children's friends.

Keep paper/pencil and/or a small whiteboard in your pantry. You could also paint a chalkboard on the back of your pantry door. You will be surprised how this will encourage family members to add what they would like to the inventory or what they have noticed is out-of-stock.

If you can't get everything into the pantry neatly, you might store non-essential items in a more "remote" storage location such as the garage or basement.

Basic Pantry Staples:

Baking Soda Baking Powder Corn Starch Flour Sugar (Powdered, Granulated and Brown) Yeast Stock (Chicken,

Beef, Vegetable) Maple Syrup Cooking Wine Milk Butter Eggs Mustard Lemons (or Lemon Juice) Mayonnaise Garlic Hot Sauce Onions Parmesan cheese

Other Handy Pantry Items:

Dried Beans Pastas Spaghetti Sauce Canned Soup (Cream of Chicken or Mushroom) Various Cheeses Sour Cream Cream Cheese Frozen Vegetables (usually frozen taste better) Potatoes Celery Carrots

Happy Pantrying!

Children's Bedroom Detox

Achild's room is disorganized either because of a lack of knowledge and know-how by the child, or by choice. A child is naturally full of curiosity and naturally places items in the most convenient place for them, so that they can get to their next curiosity... and the cycle continues. Therefore, a child will keep a cluttered lifestyle until they know better and until it serves them better to do otherwise. To keep a child's room organized, the child needs the tools and the know-how to organize; this is where the parent comes in.

The Approach: Choice and Reward Within

As a parent, it is important to guide the child without criticizing, but instead with positive reinforcement that allows your child to find the reward from within. This allows the child to learn to choose an organized lifestyle for their own personal reasons -- instead of for external reasons. For example, if they are keeping an organized room because of a promised treat or gift, or because it makes the parent happy, what happens when those rewards are not present? The child should take care of his or her responsibilities because it makes them happy.

Now, this doesn't mean that you can't withhold a daily treat or a weekly gift if your child doesn't take care of responsibilities. This is like "real life": if you don't go to work, you don't get paid; if you don't pay your electric bill, you don't get electricity. They need to know that these consistent items are earned, like a paycheck for adults. If the child has television or video game time at a certain time every day, they should get to have this at the same time every time, unless they haven't earned it.

Note however, that this is not a reward, but a normal consistent item that the child receives for doing a normal consistent behavior. They are not getting a treat for cleaning their room or punished for not cleaning their room; they basically get what they get. So, when they ask (and they should ask) for their television time, you ask, "Is your room done?" -- letting them answer their own question. If they don't want to clean their room, then they don't want to play video games, watch T.V., or have their daily treat. It's all about choice.

It is also very important to not be critical, but instead to praise the child when they do a good job. Let the child find the reward from within. The child should get responses that let them know that they should be happy with their own self and not happy because mommy and daddy are happy. For example, you can say, "You did it. You put your toys away all by yourself!" or "You are so good at (blank)." A response like "good girl" is a response that leaves the child's self-esteem dependent on the response, instead of the action or behavior. They begin to look for these general responses, to know that they are good in your eyes. By following these steps consistently, your child will make the choice to be organized.

The Approach: Routines and Consistency

The parent needs to consistently help the child get organized. Show and teach your child the routines necessary to take responsibility for their own area and to keep organized. It is important that the training is done everyday and that the kid is held responsible everyday. Start small and make sure the child understands what needs to be done before holding the child accountable. It begins with showing how to put things away, and then by guiding the child, and then by taking off the training wheels. For example, start with having your child put their dirty clothes in the hamper, reminding the child to do so, and then holding the child accountable. Consistency and routine is the key to having your child consistently stay organized.

Tools:

This starts with giving your child the tools to organize. The tools give the child a consistent place for items to go and the ability to put things away. These are some tools the child should have:

Closet Doubler

- These extra closet rods hook onto an existing rod to create a double hang feature. This brings the closet rod down to their level

Hooks mounted at a height the child can reach

- Some clothing like jackets and sweaters, that don't need to be washed every time they are worn, can be hung on hooks.

Clear shoe boxes

- Use clear shoe boxes to store shoes that are not being worn the next day.

Labeled or colored bins or boxes

- Use boxes and bins that are labeled with a picture of the items that go in the bin.
- Use boxes and bins that are colored to organize similar items. For example, toys in a blue bin, books in a white one, crafts in a red one, and so on.
  Hamper without a lid

- Keep a hamper out in the open (out of the closet) in the child's room
  A check list (for school age)

- Helps prioritize.

Using the Tools:

Then the child needs to learn to use the tools. Here are some methods to show your child how to organize (remember consistency is the key):

Preparing for the next day

- Have your child choose their clothing from their closet and place it on a designated hook.
- Have your child place their shoes for the next day under the bed or with the next day's outfit. All shoes not being used currently, or for the next day, should be in clear stackable shoe boxes.
- Have your child prepare their backpack for school and place on the hook.

  Arriving back at home

- Have your child put their jacket, backpack, and hat on designated hooks
- Have your child tell you or write it down in their to-do-list what they will be doing (i.e. snack time, then homework, video games, play outside, shower, clean up, get ready for tomorrow, and sleep). (This will teach prioritizing and instill the normal routines that should happen if responsibilities are achieved.)

Annual Purging

Use Christmas or another day the child receives new items as a motivator for making decisions to make room for new items. Ask them which items they would like to give to a sibling, friend, or a family in need. Don't force the issue; just let the child know that if they don't have the shelf space, they don't have the room for a new item.

If you teach your child how to organize and teach them how to take responsibility for their own area, it will traverse from the bedroom to school, work, and life in general. Stay consistent and eventually your child will do the same. It may be a hard road, but laying a good foundation for your child, and saving your sanity, makes it all worth it.

Clean Out Your Closet – Straighten Out Your Life

What do you think of when you think of closets?

- Places to store your clothes and shoes?
- Places for bags and boxes
- Places to hide gifts for upcoming holidays?

- Bins and boxes of unfinished projects and forgotten purchases?

What do you think should be the characteristics of a closet?

- Clean
- Dry
- Fresh smelling-but not fragrance.
- Mold and mildew free

Is your closet packed so tight that you can't open the door? In a recent attempt to declutter, they had to have the doors put back on track before we could get into the closet. The quilts and other stuff had pushed the doors off track. The closet in the guestroom and was a great place to just put a few things out of sight...and a few more and then well, a few more until glimpses of quilts were to be seen bulging from behind the doors...except the doors were closed. That called for professional help!

Before you get to the breaking point....

I have a plan for closets that will help you that is easy to remember: C.L.E.A.N.

CLEAR it all out (clear and clean) LOOK at the space you have to actually use for storage. EVALUATE the stuff which must go in that space. ALL of it has to go somewhere and not just poked into another hiding place NEVER let it get this way again.

You will find that though this method seems simple, it will work well for you and help you conquer the closet monster before he gets control of your space

CLEAR it all Out

You may need to enlist help. Be careful that the contents do not come tumbling down on you. As you take things out of the closet, sort through and categorize the contents as you remove them. Take the clothes on hangers out and lay them across the bed neatly so they will not wrinkle...or maybe they will unwrinkle. Make a stack of things that need to go to another room. When you get ready to take a break from your work, deliver some of the things to their new location. If possible, put them their proper place as you go.

To have a complete closet experience it really needs to be clean. Get out the vacuum and go over all the surfaces. Get into the crevices. Wipe off shelves and clear out any dust bunnies from the corners.

LOOK at the Space you Have and Consider What you Need to Store in There

Will it all fit? What would help make the best use of the space? Don't do a major renovation right now, but do start to look around in the stores to see if there are some shelves and containers that you could use to make better use of the closet space you have.

Remove the things from the room that you want to give away. It makes me feel less guilty that someone can enjoy what I no longer need. As I pack up the things to give away, I make pictures of the items by laying them across a bed or couch and then itemize as I put them into the donation bag. One of my favorite parts is packing the stuff up and carting it off to donate to a worthwhile charity. Yeah! All the stuff is gone and I have a more space for the things I will really use!

EVALUATE the Piles of Stuff One by One

What needs to go back in the closet? Do you just want to store clothes and shoes? Do you have boxes of keepsakes that need a cool, dry place? Archival quality boxes make a good place for photos and you can organize them by date, subject or whatever works for you.

What clothes are you really going to wear? To really see what clothes are being worn, turn all the clothes facing to the right when you start the season. As you wear an item and replace it in the closet, turn the clothes facing the other way and move them over to the left side. At the end of the season, when it comes time to switch the clothes out, notice which ones have not been turned around to face the other way. Those are the ones which have not been worn. Of course, there are some things that are specific for special occasions or have a real sentimental value (but those should be few and be the exception). Unless there is a really good reason to keep it....toss it. Put your thinking cap on and decide the destination. Charity, garage sale (or tag sale), consignment store or take it online to auction. And folks, let's admit it....some things need to go in the trash bin.

We can talk about some creative ideas later on....sounds like a good topic for a teleseminar. What do you think about that? How about ways to re-purpose things that have outgrown their original use? Do you have any of those? I do.

ALL of it Needs to go Somewhere

Clutter just lying around breeds more clutter which turns to chaos and then...the cycle returns. If some of the stuff belongs to someone else, ask them to retrieve it. This is the best chance for them to rescue their belongings. Do you have children that think your home is free storage? Seriously, if it is their treasure, they will surely want to watch over it in person.

Now is the time to get out the planning notebook and make a diagram of the closet space. Jot down the measurements of all walls and shelves. I like the open wire shelving that has adjustable shelves. If you don't actually use all the rod space to hang clothes, you can install a shorter clothes rod and have room available for shelves and even pull-out drawers and trays. There is nothing that makes such a difference as customized shelving. What changes can you make in your closet design? Here is where your imagination and planning can make a real difference for years to come.

Get out the boxes, plastic bins and whatever you have to start organizing clutter into real, usable assets. Now you should have space in your closet so that you can actually see what you have to wear. Arrange outfits together or divide the clothes by item (such as pants, shirts, jackets) or by use (such as dressy, casual, sport).

Clean and refresh your clothes, shoes, etc. before putting them back in the closet. If it is worth keeping, it is worth having it in clean usable condition. Do you remember the frustration when you pulled out a clean shirt to wear only to find it had a button missing? With the new rule, that should not happen again. Do you have any socks you aren't really using? Stuff them with cedar chips from the pet store, tie off the end of the sock and then put it in your shoes to keep them fresh and clean smelling. This is a way to reduce, recycle and reuse old socks.

How many purses can you carry at once? Probably just one. If you will tuck the others in their special place in a bin or drawer, they will keep their shape and not get all banged up in the floor of the closet. You can take some tissue paper or other clean paper and stuff them lightly so they will hold their shape. Just a hint: be sure you have not left anything important in the bag before you put it up. Otherwise, there may be some frantic searching going on some morning.

The Final Step May be Last But it is Important. NEVER Let it Get This Way Again

Make a plan here that will work for you. It needs to be a good fit for the person using the space. The closet is not a place to just poke things out of sight. Those things are quickly forgotten. That costs both money and time. Have you ever bought something you really needed only to find the one you originally purchased and forgotten still in the sack from the store a few days later? Take a photo of your closet as it is now. Fresh, clean and organized. Place the photo where you can see it as a reminder of how you want to keep it looking. With just a bit of upkeep and learning to put things where they actually belong, this task will not need to be repeated.

So, no one can ask you "What's hiding in your closet?" and you not want to show them that they are now wrong. Nothing is hiding in there anymore. It's all organized and being used.

Conquer the Junk Drawer

So...What's a junk drawer? They must be something very common, with a common understanding, because we all have them - at least one! Is it a "catch-all?" A "pack rat's heaven?" Does it have a general purpose or is it just a junk collection?

A junk drawer is a reflection, a microcosm of a whole room, or your whole house, just on a smaller scale. It is generally a temporary catch-all, where things of all manner and description are tossed to just get them out of the way. But, sometimes they are there a lot longer than temporarily! These are items that just get thrown in because you don't know what to do with them (they're "homeless"); or, you don't want to take them to their "home" right now (you'll get to it later!); or, you might need "it" someday (even though you aren't even sure what "it" is!).

What exactly is clutter? What does it mean to be organized or disorganized? It is NOT neatness, being clean and tidy. Organization is being able to find what you need when you need it. Also, to get done what you need to have done when it needs to be done.

- It comes and goes, like a pendulum, depending on life's events and circumstances, good and bad (wedding vs. funeral).
- It is not a character flaw! It just IS! You just have to deal with it regularly in order to keep the "homeless" items, the unwanted items to a minimum so that they don't overwhelm you with an immensity that just grows and grows!
- It is a symptom of too much stuff with nowhere to be!

- When you see your way through all this stuff, you will feel more positive energy, more freedom and have more space surrounding you.
- What is the goal in organizing? To get it "good enough!"

Now, because a junk drawer is a microcosm of a whole room, or house, you would use the same organizing principles you would use in that larger scenario. You...

Envision and plan the space based on its purpose, what it's used for and the space available. You can even set up little "zones," like you would in a larger space. For instance, my kitchen junk drawer is a combination of the kitchen "office" and "boxed" things, such as Zip Locks, foil, plastic wrap. I have very few drawers in my kitchen, so the few I have must do "double-duty!"

PURGE!

Why do we get to this point in the first place? We generally have too much stuff! We buy-buy-buy and have no control. We don't know what we have, so we have duplicates of lots of things...because we have so much stuff that we never found a "home" for ...and thus can't remember that we already bought them! It's a vicious circle! Lots of time and money wasted! So:

1. EMPTY everything out of the drawer and give the drawer a good wiping down.

DISCARD all the garbage and broken items. Do a "quick sort" where you just go through everything very quickly for the types of items that just don't need to be dealt with.

2. SET ASIDE everything that belongs in another place. Don't go there now - just focus on the task at hand and get to that later!

SORT!

1. Initially, sort by use, or like-with-like, and put everything into various piles. What belongs here? What would fit better somewhere else in your home or shop or office?

2. There is NO right or wrong - you would sort and decide based upon what's right for YOU, and those who will also use the space.

3. You can sort by use, or category, or season, or topic.

4. Do you USE this? Where? How often? Do you LOVE it? Then, respect it and place it where you can show that you honor it!

5. Now, since this IS just a little microcosm of a bigger area, you most likely won't find things here to donate or sell,

but that's the sort of thing you would also keep in mind if you were organizing a closet or china cabinet or garage. Donating benefits in several ways: you help others; can get a tax deduction (get a receipt!); and it frees up your space.

CONTAINERIZE!

1. Find a "home" for the items you have decided to keep in this space.

2. Make sure they are in something you can see in. Make sure that containers you can't immediately see into are labeled.

3. Group items as you intend to use them, as you think of them, i.e. "office stuff", "tools", etc. based upon your preferences.

4. Repurpose other items into storage containers: old checkbook boxes, business card boxes, candy boxes. No need to go out and buy a bunch of fancy plastic dividers, at least initially. Don't ever buy until you know exactly what you need!

MAINTAIN & MODIFY

1. Whatever systems you have set up will need to have modifications and fine-tuning from time to time, as your life changes, events happen, and YOU change. What's working? What's NOT working? If you find you aren't

using the set-up you planned, then it is time to tweak your organizing system a bit to fit where you are now, so that you can be more efficient and happier in that space. Make sure you are living in the present, and that systems in your home are functioning for you IN that present.

2. Keep it up! It is better to have small, regularly-scheduled purging sessions than to wait until the drawer doesn't close anymore. Don't let your junk drawer become a junk room!

3. Maintenance isn't supposed to be fun, no more than house-keeping is! But, don't over-organize. Don't over-analyze! Keep it simple. Focus and stick to the task at hand. Do the maintenance when you have time to devote to the task and can be methodical, not hurried, but do "just good enough!"

A woman mentioned recently that she thought it was silly to have an article such as this, that a junk drawer is just a necessity of life, that everyone needs at least one! I would agree. You should have somewhere to just toss things on an interim basis, but just that! There is nothing in any of this organizing process which has anything to say about being perfect - that you cannot be! In fact, there is case in point that some disorganization is actually good for creativity, so remember the phrase "good enough!"

Keep on organizing - one step at a time. If you see a pile, deal with it! Watch out for flat surfaces - they have a tendency to collect anything and everything. If you're done with something, put it away. If you don't have any more room for certain items, it's time to begin the process of sorting and purging again. Give yourself some "buying" parameters: one thing in/one thing out, or better yet, one in/two out!

After dealing with just one little drawer, you will feel more effective, efficient, confident and in control and ready for the next project! Relax and reward yourself for accomplishing this project, then set a goal for your next one. You can use these same organizing principles in any project you choose to take on, any other drawer, surface or room!

Tackling Mount Saint Laundry

Washing clothes can feel like one of those thankless jobs that never seems to end. The dirty garments just keep coming in no matter how often you sort and fold.

Laundry room organization can make this process easier because it will help you streamline the tasks.

Building Your Own Pedestals

Pedestals under washing machines and dryers are all the rage, and for good reason. They help elevate these appliances to make them easier to use. They also provide beneficial storage where you need it the most. If you'd love to experience the advantages of pedestals, but you're not crazy about the prices, there are do-it-yourself options out there that can make this a reality. Build an enclosed shelving system out of plywood. With center supports, the shelves will be strong enough to hold the appliances. Paint the wood in a light and bright color. Use the shelves to store laundry baskets or bins when you're not using them. This shelving might be the perfect place to stow off-season garments, too.

Foldable Drying Rack

Air drying delicate items is an ongoing challenge. Improve laundry room organization with a foldable drying rack that folds up and out of the way when you're not using it. With a board fastened to the wall and a small ladder fastened at the bottom, it's a simple process to fold down the ladder for horizontal drying and push it back up again when the items are dry.

Finding Hidden Space

Effective laundry room organization is often about maximizing the space in an otherwise congested room. Look for innovative ways to find extra room, such as installing the dryer over the washing machine. As long as you have a front-loading machine, this configuration shouldn't be a problem. Use every niche in the space for storage, including space between appliances or on either side. Narrow shelves will often fit in these small areas. Shelves with casters will easily pull out and push in for access to items. Mount shelving onto the back of doors to hold cleaning products and baskets of small items.

Horizontal Surfaces

Just as in the kitchen, horizontal surfaces are an advantage in the laundry room. Consider the benefit of a countertop installed directly above a washer and dryer. You can fold items immediately as you take them out of the dryer. Don't forget to make the space as pleasant as it is functional. The addition of a backsplash behind a counter and colorful tiles on the floor will make this area much more enjoyable.

Storage

Install as many cabinets as you can fit for effective laundry room organization. Above the appliances, cupboards will hold virtually any household items, from off-season decor to backup cleaning supplies. A sink and cupboards work in conjunction with many clothes-cleaning activities, enabling you to tackle tough stains effectively. Open shelves are great for this area too when they hold large bins or baskets full of items.

Top 5 Laundry Room Questions Answered

Okay, I confess: I don't know if these are the top 5 laundry room questions in the whole world, but when I started researching organization for myself (and my teeny tiny laundry space), I saw some questions asked over and over. As long as I was curious about them anyway, I figured I'd write an article to share the answers I found.

So, without further ado, I give you the list:

Frequently Asked Laundry Room Questions

1. What's that smell and how do I get rid of it?

Laundry rooms can have funky odors. Sometimes you know what's causing them and sometimes you don't. Here are a couple of common culprits you might check into:

Septic/sewer smells -- If there are drains in the floor, shower, sink, etc. that don't see much use, try pouring water into them to fill the drain traps (these can dry out when they're not used, which allows sewer gas to enter the house).

Musty/damp smells -- It could be mold/mildew. Make sure your dryer is venting outside the house properly, and make sure there aren't leaks coming from anywhere. If there is a leak, water can get under floors and into walls where mold and mildew can thrive.

2. Can you move the laundry room upstairs (to the second or third floor)?

Sure! It's actually becoming quite popular to move laundry rooms closer to bedrooms, which are usually located upstairs. Who wants to tote baskets full of clothes up and down multiple levels of stairs?

It does cost some money and there are some hoops to run through. The washer and dryer should be installed close to existing water lines, and you'll also have to run a 220 volt electrical line in for the dryer. Building codes in your area may also require you to put in a floor drain.

3. Where can I find cheap cabinets?

Cabinets are a great way to add storage. But you don't usually see laundry room cabinets advertised as such when you visit the home improvement store. Sure, you could use some of the nice looking cabinets from the kitchen remodeling section, but those aren't going to be cheap.

One thing you can do is reuse old kitchen or bathroom cabinets and mount them on the wall in your laundry room. Check with second hand stores or even junkyards to find them. Lots of people throw out perfectly good cabinets just because they don't match their new kitchens.

4. What's an inexpensive way to organize the laundry room?

As mentioned above, cabinets offer a way to create storage that isn't out in the open. You can also save space by using ironing boards that fold up behind the door, getting laundry hampers/baskets that can be folded or otherwise compacted (i.e. mesh hampers), and adding wall-mounted hanging racks that can be pushed/folded nearly flush with the wall when they're not in use.

5. How can we save money and reduce energy costs?

People are looking for lots of way to save energy (and thus save money on monthly bills) around the house, and the laundry room is definitely a spot where improvements can be made.

If you have the money, investing in a new energy-efficient washing and drying machine can pay off in the long run, but appliances aren't cheap, so here are some other ways to save energy without spending any money:

- Only run the clothes when you have a full load
- If the weather is nice, hang your clothes out to dry
- Clean the lint trap after every load
- Avoid buying clothes that require costly dry cleaning

Bonus Question!

How can you make your own laundry detergent?

I found this recipe online and had to add it to this article (since another way to save money is to make your own detergent):

Mix...

- 1 Cup grated Fels-Naptha soap
- 1/2 Cup 20 Mule Team Borax
- 1/2 Cup Washing Soda.

Use 1-3 tablespoons per load (adjusting for load size and dirtiness).

There you have it--the top laundry room questions answered. Laundry room organization need not be lifeless or boring, once you begin seeing how order in this space will benefit the process.

Bathrooms Made for Relaxing

If your bathroom is not the relaxing retreat you've always dreamed of, but rather the drop off point for dirty laundry, half-used health and beauty products, and other clutter, then take heart! You CAN turn things around.

Start by emptying cabinets, drawers, and countertops and throwing away these items:

- Products whose expiration dates have passed.

- Old bottles of shampoo, conditioner, lotions and shaving products whose contents are virtually empty.
- Expired medicines and those intended for one time use, such as antibiotics or eye drops.
- Products that give you a rash, smell funny, or are oozing out of their tubes.
- Makeup that's old, dried, cracked and separated, or doesn't compliment your skin color.
- Bars of soap which are too small to use.
- Broken and unused appliances, like hair dryers, shavers, curling irons and straightening wands.
- Old perfumes and nail polish.
- Combs with missing teeth.
- Toothbrushes over three months old.
- Broken jewelry, earrings and cuff links without a match (they're probably hiding out with those missing socks.)

Donate these:

Unopened, unused travel soaps, shampoos, conditioners, shoe shine cloths, shower caps, sewing kits, and any other miniature-sized products you don't intend to use. Women's shelters and nursing homes love these thoughtful gifts.

Now that you've gotten down to essentials it's time to reassess your organizing strategy. In any bathroom, there's usually some combination of drawers, cabinets, and shelving. Consider adding or increasing one or more of these elements to solve tricky storage problems.

Drawers

Shallow drawers work best for storing small flat items like jewelry, makeup, hair pins, combs, hair bands, and small accessories. To keep the contents from sliding around and getting mixed together each time you open the drawer, purchase drawer organizers. One type allows you to measure, cut, and attach plastic dividers in the exact configuration you need. If you prefer a simpler method, you may opt for individual trays of various lengths, widths and depths which can be arranged and rearranged as often as necessary, or buy one large tray with several built-in, permanent compartments.

You can also purchase trays that sit on top of the drawer (inside it) that you can slide forward and backward. This offers the option of creating a "double decker" storage area. Just remember you'll have less room underneath for other items.

Deeper drawers are handy for storing larger, bulkier items and electrical appliances such as hair dryers, shavers, and styling tools. Accessories can be stored along with them in separate containers to keep them organized and neat.

Cabinets and Cupboards

For larger or taller items, cleaning supplies, or bottles containing liquids which must be stored upright, under-the-sink storage may be the best choice . Here you can keep soap refills, shampoo and conditioner, nail polish remover, hair spray, and other grooming products. If you have a pedestal sink these items can be stored in a nearby cupboard or cabinet.

To keep items from falling over when they're kept in a larger area, I like to insert a few square or rectangular plastic containers. I usually sort the contents by category, such as nail products, medicines, or hair care, so that when I want to find a certain type, I know it will be with all the others just like it. Then, I can easily pull out the container, use what I need, and put the whole thing away in one easy gesture.

This method can save valuable time in the morning when you may be in a hurry to get out the door, by reducing the time it takes to find what you need. Containerizing also allows for quicker cleanup of spills and keeps things looking neat and tidy.

If you have trouble reaching items in the back of deep cupboards or just enjoy additional convenience, you can purchase pull-out trays, racks, or bins, which are mounted on the floor of the cupboard with a few screws. They come in various sizes, are made of plastic, wire mesh, or other materials and often come with a stackable second level.

For bathrooms with minimal drawer space you can purchase multi-drawer units made from wood, wicker, plastic or metal at your favorite bath store, retail outlet or even the organizing section of your local home improvement store. These can be placed wherever you need them and often fit nicely in narrow under-utilized spaces. You can also buy smaller versions to keep on the vanity, in a cupboard, or on a shelf.

Shelves

Your shelving may consist of built-ins, an étagère over the commode, or shelves within a cupboard or cabinet. If they're moveable you'll have even greater opportunities for maximizing their usefulness.

Shelves are popular for storing towels, wash cloths, facial tissues, toilet paper, and other products which require frequent replenishing. They're also great for bottles, sprays and smaller contained items.

If your shelves are open and in full view, you can give your bathroom a beautiful, more sophisticated look by keeping smaller items in attractive containers, such as wicker baskets, lacquered boxes, glass or metal jars, or anything suits your taste. By keeping containers covered, their contents will remain discreet, and dust and moisture can be minimized.

Whatever form they're in, shelves are versatile, functional, and desirable, in any bathroom.

Increasing Storage

If you live in a home or apartment where space is limited, there are many products to help you maximize it. For the shower you can buy a caddy that fits over the shower rod, a vertical pole with mini shelves along its length, or a variety of containers attached with suction cups, in plastic or stainless steel. These provide a convenient way to hold your shampoos, shavers, and other bath essentials.

As I mentioned previously, there are many attractive free-standing cabinets and drawer units available to match any décor. You can also buy wall-mounted cabinets, shelves, and towel racks to maximize the space above your sink, along empty walls, or in that odd shaped nook.

And don't forget the almost endless choice of hooks that can be mounted on walls or added to the door when you need extra space for your family or guests.

You mentioned a bathroom retreat...Tell me more

Now that you've gotten organized and maximized your space, let's add the icing to the cake. What better place than your bathroom spa to unwind, forget about the daily annoyances and rejuvenate your body, mind, and spirit. So, what do you do if you don't have a luxurious spa tub? Even the smallest and simplest bathroom can become more inviting by implementing a few of the suggestions below.

Splurge on new towels, something thick, soft, and beautiful. Add warmth, color, and charm to the vanity by adding a small lamp surrounded by a silky ivy garland or small flower arrangement.

Replace your old or worn out shower curtain with one that's fresh and new. Don't hesitate to use something colorful or buy a rich looking fabric to enhance the beauty of the room.

Place a single large candle on a decorative holder near the vanity or tub, or if space allows, try 3-5 candles of varying heights.

The sound of trickling water is both soothing and relaxing. If you close your eyes and let your imagination blossom, a small fountain can take you miles away, making you forget you're still at home.

If aroma therapy is what you long for, add bath salts to running water to fill the room with scent.

Escape to your bathroom for a quick getaway while you soak in a foot spa or dip your hands in hot wax after a manicure treatment. Invest in a shower massage so you can experience the soothing sensations while standing in warm water.

If you prefer a long luxurious bath, rest your head on a contoured foam pillow, stretch a bath caddy across the width of the tub, and use the built in holders for your favorite book, a taper candle and glass of wine or sparkling cider.

Keep a basket filled with body wash, a natural sponge, pumice stone, bath salts and other pampering items near the tub within easy reach. Play your favorite soothing music, while you indulge yourself.

Step out of the shower or bath onto a soft Egyptian cotton bathmat and dry your skin on warm towels from the free-standing or wall mounted electric towel warmer.

Replenish your skin's moisture with rich soothing lotion from your neck to your toes. And finally, take a deep cleansing breath before you return to the world of mortals!

Purging Your Child's Toys

It happens to everyone who has children. One day you look around to realize that the toys have overtaken your house. As you step on a minuscule piece of Strawberry Shortcake's Berry Café Playset, you can't even remember the last time your daughter played with the set. You wonder how this little plastic piece ended up embedded in your foot, when the other 150 pieces have long been MIA.

You dread the next birthday or Christmas, when the mess of toys and their thousands of pieces that inevitably get lost and distributed around the house will compound and grow like some kind of mutant beast.

It's time to take action. It's time to purge the toy collection.

1. Help your kids identify their value behind why a particular toy is important to them. Then help them prioritize their values.

By prioritizing what is important to your kids and having them articulate that to you, it will help you decide how much space to devote to a particular kind of toy. Let's say, for example, that your child is nuts about dinosaurs. It just makes sense that he'd want a wide variety of dinosaurs represented, doesn't it? On the other hand, a kid who loves dolls might be convinced that it is more important to lavish love and care on a limited number of dolls-and that the rest could find good homes elsewhere. That child might need more space for doll accessories, like a crib, but can make do with 2 or 3 especially beloved dolls.

2. Have as much shelve/bin/drawer space for your child as you can spare, so that they can stay organized.

Help kids learn to categorize toys into shelves or bins. This will allow your child to see visually how much she has of one kind of thing-and in turn help her decide how much she needs of one thing. Often it is not until all of one kind of toy has been gathered into one place, for example, that a child realizes she has as much as she does. Seeing it all together helps her realize one good set of colored pencils and/or crayons, for example, makes boxes and boxes of duplicate colors superfluous and therefore a waste of space.

3. Be creative about ways to store toys when you have limited space.

It can be really worth it to find storage or display cases for the size toy you have. My sister, for example, was a big collector of porcelain animal figurines. No one was bigger than around 4" by 4" so my dad built her a grid of shallow shelves that was about a foot wide and went all the way to the ceiling. With less than a foot of floor space, she was able to safely display more than 100 figurines. Deep but narrowly spaced shelves for things like boardgames and puzzles allow kids to store long flat things on shelves that resemble big CD holders. This kind of shelving can often be found in teachers' supply catalogues. Rather than duplicating that kind of storage for each child, have a central location for similarly shaped toys. Soft things-like stuffed animals and costumes, can be hung from a series of hooks suspended from the ceiling (provide a foot stool, so children can reach up). Shelves that slide out on rollers allow you to place toys 2-3 deep, and kids can still be able to find them (especially if you think in categories, like dump trucks one behind the other, etc).

The best way to organize kids' toys is to limit the number of toys they have to the toys they actually play with and use. Tips 4-8 address how to do that!

4. As toys and arts and craft projects and science kits and the like come into the house, write a date on them with permanent marker.

Has your child given a birthday party where all 20 of his classmates bring him a gift? She opens them all, but in reality only four or five things actually get used? By putting a date on presents as they come in, you can show a child concretely how long it has been that he has not touched the toy. That can make it easier for a child to let a toy go out the door. If a child is still reluctant to let go of a toy, give a date a month out by which the child needs to use the toy. Tell him that if he doesn't use the toy in that time that, you will be donating the toy to a local charity. The key to this tip? Do NOT remind him that the month is close to being up and do not rub it in his face that you will be giving the toy away. Simply get rid of the toy, and if your child remembers about the toy AFTER the give-away date, comfort him and assure him that next time you are sure he will not let the give-away date come and go.

5. Help kids let go of toys by identifying the "best of" in the category.

Let's say that your child loves doing arts and crafts, and your shelves are filled with the remnants of half used kits. Have your child identify which of the projects provided the most fun and satisfaction and offer to get refills for that project. Let's say, for example, that your kid really loved the weaving kit she got for her birthday and she did all the projects listed in the manual, but then she ran out of supplies. The tissue paper and pipe cleaner flower kit, on the other hand, engaged her for an hour or so and hasn't been touched since. Knowing that you are going to buy more weaving supplies, might make it easy for her to say good-bye to the flower making kit (and if not, go back to the Tip #3 plan and put it in place for the flowers).

6. Put away toys that your child is not ready for or isn't likely to ever play with.

Go back to the 20 presents from a birthday party. It is very likely that you are a good judge of what your child is actually going to play with. In the chaos of the party, it is easy to "put things away" for safe keeping. If you put a bunch of the toys away, likely the out-of-sight-out-of-mind principle will apply and your child will completely forget they even got that toy. If a couple of months go by, and the child doesn't ask about it, quietly send that toy away with the next Good Will bag. Along the same lines, if your child gets a toy which looks like it will someday interest your child but is too sophisticated for him or her at the moment, put it away in a closet-and assuming that your child doesn't ask you for it in the meantime-YOU can gift it to your child when your child is old enough for it. OR you can later make it available for your child to give to one of his friends!

7. Use natural transitions, like the start of a new school year, to mark a Big Clean Out.

If tips 1-4 have not helped clear out the accumulation of clutter, apply a 10% tithe. Let your kids know that they are going to have to donate 10% of their toys to charity. They might balk at first, but this is another excellent way to get kids to prioritize and decide which, for example, of their books they absolutely must have. It will help them recognize that they still have books on their shelves that they read 2-3 years ago when they were much younger. Similarly, unless you have massive amounts of free space for enormous Lego projects, my guess is most kids will not register a 10%

reduction of their Lego blocks (They simply don't have the space to build something that would actually use all their blocks). If your kids greatly resist the idea of donating some of their toys, I highly recommend checking out the laugh-out-loud-funny Too Many Toys, a delightful picture book by David Shannon.

8. Help keep toys organized by making some clear guidelines about how many gifts can come into the house. Share your value with your kids that they not equate stuff with happiness or security. Help them see the value of fewer treasured objects by encouraging more thoughtful gift giving. Let relatives know that less is more-or perhaps ask relatives if they would like to go in on a gift together. Some toys, like a fancy model kit, for example a) can be quite pricey and b) actually requires extra supplies-like glue, additional paint, a big board the project can be done on so that as it is being worked on it can be slid in and out from under a bed. Relatives who think of the big picture could go in on all the pieces together. That way one gift comes into the house instead of 6-7.

You can also enlist help from close family friends and relatives by asking that they provide your child experiences rather than toys that will add to the clutter. Perhaps your daughter's best friend's family will invite her to go to the zoo with them the next time they go. Perhaps your son's uncle will take him to a hockey game. These gifts work on so many levels: They say to your child I am valued, People like having me around. They give your child time with another caring adult, so you are creating that larger safety net. The activity itself is often memorable--especially if it is in the child's honor. Again, these are great opportunities for families to go in together on an outing that might be more expensive: Grandpa can pay for the ticket, Uncle can actually get the child to the game, Aunt-who-lives-far-away can provide a gift certificate for cotton candy or a souvenir.

How to Let Your Children Keep Their Toys Willingly

Ever had problems getting your kids to keep their toys? I used to think that to get children to keep their toys after play is as hard as asking them to climb up a ladder hands-free.

My mindset was completely changed after working at the child care centre. It is a matter of making it into a habit, a routine, a die-die-must-do task. The key of the game - never do it like a chore.

1. Get 1 Or 2 Big Storage Boxes or Containers Just for Their Toys

When the toys can no longer stay in the box, even after trying their balancing skills in plying them up above the edge of the box, its time to throw.

Make it a practice to throw away toys that they hardly play with just before their birthdays. All parents know how easily toys pile up after each birthday celebration.

Be careful when it comes to throwing toys away. Never ever throw away a toy the child insists on keeping. Always ask, "Shall we throw this away?" Some may say, "Children want to keep All their toys." That is not true.

Once the guideline is set and the children understand the reason for throwing some toys away; they willingly pick out toys they are not interested in playing with anymore. When there are fewer toys around to keep, it looks less tedious to the kids.

2. Get Them to Sing "the Barney Clean Up Song"

This less than 10 seconds song somehow has a magical touch. The more times the children sing, the faster their hands move. Who knows? Maybe this 20 year old Purple Dinosaur (just got to know that Barney is celebrating its 20th anniversary this year) does create songs that stimulate the kids' mind.

3. Do the Countdown

This is best when you need them to speed up and when the mess spreads across the ENTIRE HOUSE! Usually a 10-count should do the job, but if there are small pieces like jigsaw puzzles and Lego, then (to be fair) give a 20 or even a 30-count.

4. Never Help your Children

Always guide them, "Ok, after you have kept the cars, pick up the race-tracks." Helping your kids will either cause them to slacken and/or create a mindset of "Mommy will keep it herself or for me, anyway."

5. Never Say, "I'll Come Back and Check on You"

Though not helping with your hands, it is important that you sit through the whole process with them. To the kids, they are doing it because you told them to and simply because they love you. So if you disappear to do your laundry or read the newspapers, they would feel that their effort is not appreciated.

Keeping toys by themselves, indirectly teaches them a very important virtue - responsibility. You play, you keep. You mess up, you clean up. Being accountable for your actions is one very valuable lesson.

6. Be Generous With your Compliments

When your kids do what was instructed, say "Good Boy or Girl!"

When they choose to use both hands to pick up more than just 1 toy at a time, praise them, "That's clever, you pick up so many toys at a time."

When you can tell that they are feeling the strain or not motivated, encourage them, "You are doing very well."

When they start to throw a tantrum in the middle of it, encourage them, "You are doing great, I am so proud of you, it is almost done. Just a few more pieces over here."

Try not to keep saying the same words like, "Good boy or girl" throughout the whole process. Kids like to hear new stuff, so be creative with your compliments.

7. When the Children Have Completed the Whole Process, Praise Them "Good Job"

Look at the whole place now, it is so clean and neat. You kept them so fast. Now everyone can walk around without the fear of stepping on the toys, damaging them and hurting their feet. I am so proud of you."

It is very important to point to the kids the significant difference before and after. Keywords like 'clean', 'neat' and 'fast' will stay in the children's brain as the basic criteria they should maintain for the next round.

It is also a must to let your children know that what they did, do not only pleases you alone, it makes everyone else happy. This trains their mind to think of others in their actions.

Toys being the main part of their daily enjoyment, by saying the above sentence, you make known to them that their favourite toy is in danger of getting 'hurt' too, if the toy is left lying around. They would want to 'protect' their toys from harm and hence remember to keep them after play.

8. When All the Toys are Kept, Always Say, "I Am So Proud of You"

It is often good to give a small reward. Be it a hug, a kiss, a tiny M&M chocolate, a drink that they like or whatever that pleases the little ones. Rule of the thumb - never promise to give the reward before the task is assigned. This will give them the wrong motivational factor.

9. Never request your children to do it when they are in a bad mood, feeling tired or are in the mist of throwing a tantrum. You think they will cooperate? Not a chance!

10. Make if Fun

Find a big cardboard. You can help by holding the cardboard and tilting it to create a slide where the landing area is the toy box. Now your kids can put all the toys which they picked up from the floor and slide them down into the toy box. Now it has became a game and they will love it!

11. As for the next playtime, suggest that your kids keep whatever they are playing at that moment first, before they bring out another toy from the toy box.

This is not a must because such rule limits the children's creativity in playing in a different way by combining different toys together.

To sum up the pointers, get your children to keep their toys at a time when they are in a relax mood, stick through it with them with lots of praises and make them feel their effort is worthwhile by giving a reward at the end.

Keeping Up with Kids Clothes

Y ou know the saying, "Keeping up with the Jones'". Well most moms feel the same way about keeping up with kids' clothes. They grow so fast and a good share of time and money went into purchasing those clothes. There's no wonder why we'd like to save the clothes for the next child. It just makes sense. Here are some ideas for how to make that process easier.

If clothes won't be passed down to younger siblings, place a bag or box in your child's closet, room, or under the bed. As they outgrow clothes, toss the clothes right into the donation collector. Once full, take the donations to a charity and repeat the process.

If clothes will be passed down to younger siblings, place a Rubbermaid container somewhere in their room and start to fill it. Or if there's no room for a container in purge out their clothes twice a year by grabbing a Rubbermaid container sitting in basement or attic storage and return it to storage of course after filling it.

Remember these two key items as you save clothes for sibling.

1. LABEL the container with the size (not age of the child) of the clothes. Each child will reach a certain size at a different age so it's better to stick with organizing by size.

2. LIMIT how many containers you fill. Try to fill only per year for that size(s)! Yes, I know that may seem impossible, but one container of clothes for that size will be plenty. Chances are some clothes might be outdated by the time the younger sibling gets to wearing them and you might end up shopping for some new clothes for the younger sibling instead giving her or him only hand me downs.

To have another baby or not to? That is the question. Of course that's a common scenario when you're just not sure if you will or will not have another baby. So make it easy on yourself by getting the baby clothes organized now. Designate three bins- one for boy clothes, girl clothes, and one for gender neutral. You'll be all set when you do have a baby. And if you find out the baby gender you'll know what to keep versus donate.

Some parents do the sorting and purging in the laundry room as they fold clothes and do wash. Three benefits arise from doing your purging and storing there.

1. You have more room to spread out and store bins of clothes
2. The clothes are clean when you donate them.
3. You reduce your work load because you won't be folding or putting away clothes that don't fit.

The final and most important tip is to maintain the system. That's always the most important step of all. We, parents and organizers, can put a lot of systems with good intentions in place but if the systems aren't maintained they're bound to fail. So take some time to think through which system or set up would be best for your family and that would work with your time. Then start taking the steps to implement it.

Save Your Family Legacy Forever!

Holiday memories need to be preserved - along with all those other photos you have taken over the years. I have had a few questions lately on my "Ask Robin" blog about preserving your photographs and if there are any scrapbooking supplies that can be used to help those photos last longer.

Photo preservation is a huge topic out there, especially because many of us have seen our ancestors' photos yellow or deteriorate over time. So what can we do as scrapbookers to keep that from happening? Along with being a scrapbooker, I am also a photographer by trade and have some experience in this area. I have put together a list of the top ways that will keep those photos preserved for years to come!

1. Use acid free everything on your scrapbooking pages. Yes, acid free is a big deal. Many of those photos you see that have yellowed, cracked, or faded have done so because of the acid in the paper used and the acid in the albums they have been kept in.

2. Use sheet protectors to separate photos. Even if you never scrapbook your photos, you should always keep them separated and protected. Also, why print a photo if you are not going to look at it or reminisce? If you haven't scrapbooked the photo yet (and don't plan on doing so within the next few years), putting it in a photo album with acid free sleeves is the way to go. Stay away from any of the sticky albums that use adhesive to hold the picture down or are "magnetic". These albums tend to be highly acidic and dangerous to photos.

3. Print photos on "permanent paper" or paper that is acid-free, lignin free, and pH neutral. Just check the labels before buying paper - even some photograph paper isn't suited for long-term photo preservation. Of course, if you have a store or company print them, you shouldn't have to worry. But you may want to ask about the paper they print on and the ink they use to make sure it is acid free.

4. Use acid-free ink with your inkjet for printing photos. As a general rule, most inkjet printers use acid-free ink, but some do not. Make sure you check with your manufacturer to see if their ink is acid free. Many companies also make statements about their ink and how fade resistant it is. If you do use an inkjet printer and want the images to stay vibrant - keep all images out of direct light and keep all images away from water or liquids.

5. Acid-free photo boxes can be safe as well. Just keep in mind that photos can stick together if moisture gets into them. The best way to preserve them in this method is to separate them with acid-free envelopes or sleeves.

6. When labeling photos, always use acid-free ink and/or labels. Most regular ballpoint pens can eventually bleed through your photos or onto other items. If you will not be scrapbooking your photos, an acid-free, smudge proof pen/marker would be the easiest option. And if you are like me (overly organized and neat), you can print onto acid-free labels and adhere them to the photo.

7. Coating your prints with veneers or sprays can be a solution - especially for those photos you have on display. For example, I have a family photo that has been framed without a mat and glass for protection. I had it sprayed with a UV protection spray (UV resistant fixative) at my local photo lab (not all labs will do this), but you can buy the spray at photo supply stores or online. I have had the photo on the wall for 4 years now and there doesn't appear to be any fading and it can easily be wiped down for dust particles. I have also found some water-based varnishes that do a similar task and are also supposed to protect against the yellowing effect. I found one at inkjetart.com . Although these topcoat sprays and such are a solution, many of the product labels say that they are not a permanent protection, but they can help your photos last longer and protect against some environmental factors.

8. Always keep a copy of your photos on other types of media. After I have printed my photos, I always burn them to a CD or DVD. Although there are some critics out there that will argue that CD/DVD's won't last forever, I believe that if needed in the distant future, I can convert my CD into whatever the new media is at that time. I then store these photo CD/DVD's in protective cases and boxes (make sure to label them!). As a scrapbooker, I also like to include CD's with some of my scrapbooking

layouts - especially if I took 100's of photos for one occasion and don't want to print all of them.

9. Give copies to other people! If you have a flood, hurricane, fire, etc. there really is no way to know if your photos will survive, unless you have shared them with others. Go photo-happy and send your photos to relatives and friends. I know that my mom has sent most of the kids in the family treasured photographic prints and CD/DVD's with photos and recordings. If she were ever to lose her treasured memories in a fire, she would probably be able to recover most of them from us. Don't have a lot of family and friends (I sure hope that is not you!)? Another option is to use an online photo storage website. There are many free or very inexpensive sites out there - check out myphotoalbum.com, kodakgallery.com, and shutterfly.com. The great advantage to these sites is that you can share your photos too.

10. Store your scrapbooking albums, photo boxes, digital media, and photos in environmentally safe places. Remember that light, moisture, and temperature can harm your photos. The garage or cold storage room may not be the best place for your photos. A dark closet that keeps the same temperature most of the time would be a better choice.

Put an End to the Accessory Madness

I t has happened a million times. You are all dressed up for an important meeting, but are running late for work. In a frenzy, you start rummaging through your accessories for that perfect pair of earrings, but alas, you can only find one. Your jewelry drawer is as big of a black hole as that sock-eating clothes dryer.

Thankfully, there are a wide range of organizers that can help solve this daily dilemma of missing jewelry. They range from classic tabletop designs to wall mounts, closet storage versions and even ones that hang over a door. So say goodbye to missing jewelry and save the one earring look for the pirates of the Caribbean. These jewelry organizers will make accessorizing a breeze.

Tabletop Organizers

Fans of traditional tabletop jewelry boxes have many choices to choose from. These are grown-up versions of the ballerina jewelry boxes of your youth, with sleek designs and numerous compartments to keep your collection organized. Two boxes worth checking out are the 3 - Drawer Java Organizer and the Spinning Mirror Jewelry Organizer.

The 3- Drawer Java Jewelry Organizer is perfect for large collections, with 3 large storage compartments for all types of jewelry. The box measures 10 3/4 x 7 x 6 inches and opens to reveal a mirror and four divided sections. The middle storage compartment is completely open for items like bracelets and watches. The bottom section is also open for other jewelry or keepsakes.

For a more upright tabletop model, the Spinning-Mirror Jewelry Organizer features three mirrored doors that spin around to reveal a cup to hold rings or earrings and five plated hooks for bracelets or necklaces. This spinning

organizer is made of wood and glass and measures in at 10 x
2 1/2 x 13 inches.

Wall Mounted Organizers

If a lack of counter space is a concern, a more appealing
option is a wall mounted jewelry organizer. These come in
fancy styles suitable for display in any room, or plainer styles
for areas like bedrooms or walk-in closets.

For people who want a jewelry organizer they can display,
the Oak Mirror Jewelry Armoire is a beautiful choice. The
armoire has an oak veneer finish with crown carved applique
and a mirrored front. It measures 36 1/4 x 20 x 7 1/2 inches,
making it an excellent organizer for large collections. When
you open the armoire, there are a variety of storage options,
including hooks and felt compartments, which means an end
to tangled necklaces and missing earrings.

If an upscale wall mounted jewelry organizer is a bit dear for
your budget, a no-frills option is the fittingly generically
named Wall Mount Jewelry Organizer! But, despite the
simple moniker, this workhorse of a product gets the job
done with specially designed holes and slots that can hold up
to 42 pairs of earrings! Necklace pegs also come in handy to
keep tangles at bay. Made of wood, the wall mount organizer

measures 18 x 7 1/2 x 3/16 inches and comes with mounting hardware.

In-Closet and Over Door Organizers

In- closet and over door jewelry organizers are perfect for people who like to keep their jewelry tucked away and not on display. The Ultra Jewelry Organizer is a convenient option that is a double-sided vinyl organizer that hangs from your closet rod with a built-in hanger. This model has 37 compartments with clear pockets, to make finding what you are looking for a breeze. The Ultra measure 26 3/4 x 13 inches.

If adding another item to your already jammed closet rod is completely out of the question, the Over Door Jewelry Organizer is a better option. This organizer has hooks that hold over 300 items, including up to 75 pairs of earrings, 75 bracelets or watches, 50 rings and 16 necklaces. Made of powder-coated steel, the Over Door Jewelry Organizer measures in at 21 1/2 x 4 x 31 inches. This item can also be wall mounted and hardware for that purpose is included.

For a fancier over door option, the Over Door Mirror and Jewelry Armoire is a good choice. This organizer has a shatterproof mirror door that opens to a variety of slots, hooks and compartments that hold up to 96 rings, 48 earrings and 36 necklaces. It is made of wood and measures 48 x 14 x 40 inches.

With so many types of jewelry organizers available, there is bound to be one that fits any size collection. Whether your preference is a display piece or one that you can tuck away in a closet, the options are limitless. So say goodbye to single earrings and tangled necklaces for good with an organizer that keeps your jewelry collection safe, secure and easy to navigate

Kitchen Savvy Leads To Abundance

Kitchen organization doesn't have to be hard or time-consuming and the effort is so worth it. An organized kitchen makes both cooking and entertaining a pleasure. Instead of searching through cupboards and drawers for different items, taking a little time on a regular basis, keeps your kitchen organized. The trick to an kitchen organization is simply incorporating these 8 simple tips and ideas and your kitchen will run more efficiently, it will look more like a kitchen seen in a decor magazine. When it comes to kitchen organization I use the 3Es of organization and they are Easy, Effective and Efficient. Within each of these tips one or all three of these guidelines are included keeping clutter at bay.

1. Stove Area More Effective:

All great chefs have their 'go to' items within easy reach of the stove top. Depending on which items you use regularly are the items you need to consider for easy access. For instance, if the area near your stove is littered with bottles of oil, salt and pepper mills, spices, then consider keeping all these 'go to' items on a tray. The tray need not be fancy or expensive. A simple tray works well and, it can be utilitarian or decorative, your choice to fit your decor. This way, everything will be in one easily accessible place and spills, which do happen, will be easier to clean too. Think of the area around the stove as the 'tool belt' for cooking. With a tool belt you want the most used items available. Using a tray for these items helps keep your kitchen organization effective.

2. Pots and Pans Hung for More Efficient Use of Kitchen Real Estate:

Have you seen photos of chefs in their kitchens and how they often hang their pots and pans? Well, you create the same thing in your kitchen. You don't need a large area to do this; a small corner or free ceiling space close to the stove will work. I recently saw an old latter suspended over an island with S-hooks screwed into the rails making a creative and efficient way to store your pots and pans. Another way is install a handrail against a wall and then use several S-hooks to hang your pots and pans. Both these out of cupboard ideas make your pots and pans more accessible, will free up cupboard space while making a decorative statement.

3. A Clutter Free Sink Area Made Easy:

Don't you find that the around and under the sink area has become a depot for tools for scrubbing, moisturize lotions and hand soaps of different varieties. Better kitchen organization can be accomplished with the use of pretty trays or small containers where you can place your brushes and sponges. It is best to keep cleaning and scrubbing items under your sink within a container for easy and less clutter around the sink. Your hand soap will look better in a simple clear glass dispenser. This makes this utilitarian item more attractive. All these items can be purchased at very reasonable cost from local home decor or hardware stores. You don't need a lot of money to accomplish this suggestion.

These will give your kitchen sink a more uncluttered and unified look.

4. Recycling Can be Pretty Easy and Efficient:

Today recycling is part of our lives and incorporating this can sometimes be a challenge. There are lots of pull out trash bins which hold more multiple bins to make sorting easy. If this isn't an option for you, create a corner using uniform attractive containers or baskets to collect all your paper, glass, aluminum and wastes. Labeling each makes it easy for everyone in the household to keep things organized and know where each of the different trash belongs. These will look more attractive than piles of trash in your kitchen.

5. Add Some Spice to Your Spices:

When storing spices and condiments, you could try storing them all in glass jars or canning jars. These make them look uniform compared to storing them in their actual packaging. This suggestion takes a little time investment however, the benefit can be great if you think uniformity. With uniformity, you can easily keep spice jars on a tiered shelf made for either a shelf or drawer. Uniformity among spices saves space and money. Once the spice is in the jar then buying refills in bulk is less expensive. You can even label each spice easily. Think again, which spices do you use on a regular basis? Place these important spices at the front of your cupboard or drawer.

6. Failure to Prune

Do it regularly. I recommend the 3Es of kitchen organizing - make it EASY, EFFICIENT and EFFECTIVE and regular decluttering, even 10 minute chunks work. Who can't commit to pruning for 10 minutes a day or even once per week??

7. Set up a Plan or Functional Areas in your Kitchen

Cupboard and drawers become so much more functional when they are organized with one, maybe two, purposes. Junk drawers have their name for a good reason because when an area doesn't have a single purpose this is the result over time. Keep this in mind when you are looking to expand your existing space or getting more use from a cupboard or drawer. We often make the mistake that making a space function for multiple uses is better; in fact this often leads to the purpose getting muddled up and becoming disorganized.

8. Emotional Attachment

Kitchen organization doesn't need to be difficult. One thing that gets in the way is our emotional attachment to our stuff we received as gifts or inherited. If it is something that means a lot to you, don't keep it stuffed away in a drawer or cupboard - bring it out and showcase it as decoration. There are oodles of ways to accomplish this. One simple way is find an existing shelf or space to put it on. Keep this to a minimum. Too much looks too cluttered.

There you have it. Easy, Effective and Efficient tips on creating a kitchen you will love working and entertaining in. The key to kitchen organization is taking the time to do it.

Excellent Ways to Keep 'Hobby Clutter' In Check

Though hobbies can be really fun, they can also develop a huge amount of disorder and clutter. Craft projects, training booklets, as well as other miscellaneous craft materials can often take control of your home, that is, unless you have the ability to strategize a good organization plan. If you are beginning to feel the crunch of too many hobby materials, here are some tips you can use to get "hobby clutter" completely under control.

Storage is Key

Having the correct techniques for storing things as well as the ideal containers is very significant when it comes to arranging all of your hobby supplies. Luckily, there happen to be many options for storage that you can use for nearly everything that needs to be sorted. Sometimes you will be able to purchase containers that are specifically designed for particular hobby items, such as books for stamps, paper storage containers for scrapbooking, or compartmentalized organizers for things like beads and other small craft supplies. When you are selecting the correct storage container for your supplies, be sure to consider the dimensions you need, as well as the features you will find useful for your purpose. For example, if you work on your scrapbooking hobby exclusively in your craft room, a large storage cabinet could be the perfect choice. Although, if you frequently go to scrapbooking parties, you may want a more portable storage container to accommodate your needs. In order for a storage solution to be effective, it has to be easy to use and well suited to your needs.

Don't Hide What You Can Exhibit

It really does not make good sense to store things that you can effortlessly display. For instance, if you are a collector of post cards, displaying them in picture frames can be a great way to enjoy some of them. Or, if you enjoy looking at your memorabilia but do not like to leave them out on general display, try taking some digital photos of them. As soon as you have an assortment of photos that you are happy with, you can upload them to a digital photo frame specially designed to loop through all of the pictures, which you may then display on a shelf. If you gather seashells, use some to create beautiful crafts that you can use to decorate your home. Picture frames may also be useful for picture collections, baseball card collections, stamp collections, and more.

Creating Effective Work Areas

Sometimes the only reason an area becomes cluttered is because your work area is simply ineffective. If you happen to be the fortunate owner of an additional room that you have the ability to devote especially to your hobby, then you will be able to organize a work area or work surface that will allow you to possess plenty of space to work in. You might be surprised just how much more enjoyable your hobby is if you no longer have to store things away every time the family needs to use the dining room table. Organizer containers, filing cabinets, storage bins and wall shelves can all be useful for helping keep supplies neatly under control. And if your activity often gets somewhat messy, make sure that you preserve the floor and the surface of the table if you need to do so to prevent unneeded mess, and also have a garbage can on hand.

Using Magazine Racks to Keep Hobby Items Organized

When shopping for hobby supplies, such as craft books, pamphlets and instruction sheets, it is common to select these items from a magazine rack in the store, which has been neatly organized so that you can find just the book you need.

This same method that makes things so easy at the store can also be adapted in your home. Instead of storing these types of items in boxes or bookshelves, a wall-mounted magazine display rack, mounted to one wall in your office or craft room, can help you keep your craft books organized, and always accessible.

Using this method, you can label individual compartments of the magazine rack with the name of a type of craft, or perhaps with the name of a particular project you are working on. This way, if you are working on a number of projects at the same time, you can easily locate the items you need for the craft you are currently working on.

If you use the type of magazine rack that has solid, clear plastic compartments instead of a more open construction, you can also store additional small craft supplies associated with the craft project in the compartment as well. You will save time, keep your craft room neat and organized, and reduce the stress and confusion caused by constantly trying to locate the books, instructions and supplies you need for your projects.

If you choose the clear plastic variety of magazine rack for this purpose, there are a couple of types that you can select from, each having their own advantages. Some of them are considered "full view", which means that the entire front of each individual compartment is visible, without there being any overlap with the other compartments. This can be handy so that you can keep everything in full view, but this type of magazine rack will take up much more wall space.

The other type of magazine rack that is available is an "overlap" style. This style can save you considerable wall space, and gives you many more individual compartments per square foot of space. However, the entire front of each compartment isn't visible, except on the front row, and instead you can only see the top edges of the other compartments.

Depending on your usage, available wall space and storage priorities, either one of these magazine rack styles may be just what you need to keep your craft room better organized.

Having best magazine rack and any kind of chest will keep your home organized and in order. This is an important thing especially if you have young children.

Be a Garage Organizer!

How do you know it's time to get the garage in order? When people marvel that you're able to get the car into that narrow pathway in a wall-to-wall sea of boxes, tools, ladders, fertilizer bags and holiday decorations, aka "the garage," it might be time to organize. When it's December and you finally locate the Halloween decorations...again, it might be time to organize the garage. When the squirrel family is looking for new lodging with more square footage...it's definitely time to organize the garage.

Step One

Take everything, repeat everything, out of the garage. This includes every can, every bottle, every last nail. Sort things on the driveway in three labeled piles: KEEP, TRASH and DONATE/SELL. Be sure to get rid of anything you no longer use. When you have two children, do you really need eight bicycles? Donating to a charity is a great way to teach children to share their possessions with less fortunate children. If you have a family heirloom that you love too much to throw away, find a new use for it. An old wagon that Grandpa built can be painted and taken into a bedroom for displaying stuffed animals or storing books and toys. Once everything is sorted, the process will move more quickly.

Step Two

The next step is a fresh coat of paint on interior surfaces. A lighter color paint will create the illusion of more space; a light, metallic gray, for instance, on walls and ceiling will brighten the area. The floor can be painted with a heavy-duty garage floor coating, or covered in thick vinyl/rubber sheeting made specifically for garage floors, applied with two-sided adhesive tape. Another flooring option is modular garage floor tile.

Step Three

Garages are meant for cars, but the space serves many other roles, including workshop, potting barn, auto supply station and year-round storage area. The secret is to utilize vertical space. Storing as many items as possible off the floor is the best way to create a clutter-free garage.

A wall-mounted track, screwed to the wall, is an ideal system. One track can be installed approximately 7 feet from the floor for long handled items such as a broom, shovel, rake, electric trimmer, lawn furniture and ladders. Another track can be installed approximately 3 feet from the floor. This is a good place for hoses, sprinklers, dustpan and brush.

Tracking systems can be equipped with hooks, shelves, drawer units and baskets for hand tools, garden supplies, cleaning essentials. Designate one basket or drawer for carpentry tools such as hammer, pliers, wire clipper, jars of nails and screws. A metal receptacle can be included for trash, and another could be used to keep rock salt handy for icy mornings in the winter.

A pegboard with hooks and accessories is another good wall system. Any wall-storage method that keeps items of the garage floor is a valuable organizational tool.

Open-frame walls are perfect locations for small shelves. Ledges can be installed over windows and doors for seldom used items such as lanterns and other seasonal garden items.

Step Four

Find a convenient corner to use for a potting station. An ideal spot would be near a sunny window that overlooks the garden. Near a doorway is also a good location for easy hauling in and out of heavy potted plants. A potting station also needs to be close to a water supply, either use a long garden hose connected to an exterior spigot, or a four-gallon metal watering can that can be transported easily. The area will be busiest in spring and summer, but when the weather is cold, the area can be used for tending to houseplants, storing bulbs or planting and cultivating seeds.

Hang metal buckets or wire baskets on walls to hold garden twine, scissors, and plant markers. Larger items, such as hedge clippers and pruners can be hung on the wall on hooks. Equipment such as rotary spreader and wheel barrow can be hung on large hooks and held again the wall with bungee chord, with the lawn mower stored beneath on the floor. Bins on casters, either galvanized metal or plastic, are perfect for storing bulky quantities of fertilizer, grass seed and potting soil.

A potting station needs a work surface. A table or desk is one option; another is a table-top without legs attached to the wall with a hinged bracket. When the surface is not being used it can be dropped down against the wall, out of the way.

Step Five

Create a storage wall for holiday decorations, bulk grocery purchases, seasonal items and sporting equipment. A long, high shelf is the perfect place for the picnic basket and cooler or fishing tackle and rods. Shelves on the wall can be used to store household items bought in bulk, such as bottled water, rolls of paper towel, cleaning supplies, and dry food. A substitute for shelving would be a metal cabinet. Another cabinet without shelves, or a portable closet, can be used to store golf bags.

Underneath the shelving (or alongside the storage cabinet), a painted, pine storage chest with bins inside is perfect for balls, roller-blades, or helmets. Equipment can be sorted by family member or season. This is also a good location for recycle bins for plastic, metal and glass, plus a wire basket and twine for newspapers.

Bicycles can be hung on hefty hooks on the wall; or suspended from ceiling-mounted hooks. Another good location for the hooks is on a center support beam; one support beam can accommodate two bicycles.

A separate closet or metal cabinet can be designated for holiday decorations, stored according to season. Shelving is also an option if everything is stored in separate bins.

Finally, with a place for everything and everything in its place your garage will be a daily convenience and source of pride. There'll be no more wasting precious time searching and not finding. Instead, you'll know exactly where to find what you need for work or play. Once organized, you can say farewell to clutter and hello to a more pleasant lifestyle....and you car will finally no longer feel like an intruder in its own home.

Tips That Will Make Hanging Artwork on the Wall Easier

Hanging art has been and still remains an integral part of adorning our modern day man caves. We have always had an urge to make art an important element of our interiors dating as far back as the prehistoric wall cave paintings and base relief of the Egyptian tombs. Anthropologists have said ancient people thought art was magic that transported you from the mundane to the transcendent. I have to agree, because surprisingly, what we take in visually stays with us unconsciously, capturing us, and magically whisk us away to another place and time.

There are clues that will help you zero in on the type of artwork that compliments the scale and color of the room. Keep in mind the room's scheme and try to match or contrast it. Is the room neutral, pastel, or vibrantly decorated? Don't be intimidated when choosing art. It is nothing more than finding images that you like, ones that speak to you, perhaps stimulates reflection, relaxes your mind and uplifts your spirit framing your memories.

Art can be an anchor for a room's theme; it relays a story of the occupant's depth, style, humor and even their intellect. While hunting for the ideal pieces, keep in mind these images you are choosing will greet you on a daily basis. Others will be viewing it also, and the substance of your art has impact. If the impact is too much, it will drown out you theme but if it is too little, it will be lost. Discovering the art that reflects you and speaks to you can take some time to find, but once you have found the ideal pieces, how do you hang them and where?

Now that you found the coveted pieces of art, we need to find a way to properly display your artscape. This will involve identifying wall color, location, and framing/matting the artwork and then finally, highlighting each piece if needed with some accent lighting.

Wall Color:

- Consider a suitable backdrop against which to display your work.

- The wall color should not compete with your art.

- The color should either be neutral or in some way play off the colors in the art.

- Repaint the wall to compliment/accent the piece if needs be.

- Ensure back drop is smooth with unobtrusive textures.

Location:

- Allow generous amount of wall space around each work.

- Relate art to wall size- (Choose smaller pictures for narrow walls and larger works for big wall spaces.)

- Relate Art to Furniture Size (In general, when hanging art over a piece of furniture it should not be longer than the width of the furniture- a general principle being about 75% of the table's/sofa width.)

- Standard hanging height would be at eye level.

- Hang It Low-When hanging a large picture over a table for instance, the bottom of the frame should sit within 4-8" of the tabletop

- Play with size for dramatic effects-try hanging large art pieces in small spaces such as a powder room.

Hanging art in groups to make a pattern:

- Stripes- symmetrically hung in a row to create a vertical or horizontal line of art

- Plaids- a square or checkered layout

- Herringbone/diagonal- an ascending slope/stepping rows up a stairwell adds excitement to the composition.

- Mosaic- a large cluster of works together serves to display many works in a limited space.

- Artful Grid- Use of the majority of the wall with pictures that are monochromatic, same in color, same frames (if not frameless), and of the same size this will create a dramatic wall of poetry.

- One vertically hung and one horizontal being aligned at the base of the frames.

- Oversized and hung low

- Horizontal lines tend to elongate, widen, and emphasize a casual decorating scheme.

- Vertical lines tend to be more formal giving the illusion of height; it can seem more elegant and refined.

- Avoid hanging matching pictures in a perfect line whenever you'd like to emphasize a casual atmosphere.

- Symmetrical Arrangements adds balance and formality to an arrangement and is generally pleasing and calming to the observer.

- Asymmetrical Arrangements create a very eye-catching grouping and is a casual fun look for informal settings.

- Juxtapose two artworks from different periods that have a common element (color, subject matter, etc.)

- Create a collage by grouping many small artworks together linking them visually in form, theme, or color. This will allow them to play off each other creating a harmonious single graphic effect.

Framing:

- Don't choose frames/mattes that will overwhelm a piece or fails to set it off.

- Mix frames that differ stylistically and in color giving them a sense of this is a "collection".

- Try framing several items in one mat and frame.

- Varying frame shapes add interest to a picture grouping by hanging pictures with differently shaped frames.

- Pictures will have greater impact if matted in a contrasting color to the wall. Choose a dark mat for a light wall and vice versa.

- A group of pictures framed alike and hung together can have big impact.

Shelves and Alternative Wall Hangings

- Place art on a shelf creating a more dimensional effect and allows you to exhibit framed work along with other collected art, figures/pots.

- Look for objects to hang on the wall that give the impression of art such as architectural features

- Iron art is very popular and adds a great deal of interest with its 3-dimensional effect.

Accent Lighting:

Note: Beautiful artwork can be lost unless it is well lit. Illuminating the work it gives it more importance.

- The entire surface of a painting should be should be evenly lit without glare

- To light an individual piece and direct light evenly mount a picture light that has a long arm from the back of the artwork as to not damage the piece.

- Use a color correct, ultra violet-free, low wattage bulb.

- Light sculptures to enhance their forms to create a dramatic effect that cast shadows onto walls or floors.

- Use uplights and downlights of various sizes that suits each piece.

- Using track lighting above a series of pieces that perhaps run down the length of a hallway will dramatically highlight the art and light the hallway simultaneously.

- Light bookshelves and cabinets with mounted lights or clip ons

Alas, you are now armed with a holster full of new hanging art arsenal and now are officially equipped to tackle any room with your new artscaping design guidelines. Stick to your theme by supporting it with art that's repeating in colors, motifs, and style of the room's interior. Use the art as inspiration, search for pictures that move you and use their themes and colors as the foundation for other room elements. Allow the art to be humorous, fun, unexpected and whimsical. Look for themes that fit your decorating style by bringing out the colors in other elements of the room. Just remember that art endures because it releases us from repetition of habitual thought and allows us a fresh perspective; so be sure to display your work respectfully and artfully by putting some extra thought into it.

Ways to Have a Beautifully "Pet Friendly" Home

If you have pets or are considering adding them to your family in the near future, there are a lot of concerns that may come along with the addition. If you've never owned animals in the past, you may be concerned about the impact that having a pet will have on your home. If you already have a pet, you may be looking for a way to prevent any damages from happening, as well as keeping your pet's supplies organized and out of the way. By using these ten steps as guidelines, you'll be sure that your pet is safe and your home is organized.

1. One of the most frequented areas in the home by pets is the kitchen. Your dog has to eat everyday, so keeping food in a convenient location, as well as out of the way for you, will make things much easier on a daily basis. A great way to store food conveniently and disguise it in a decorative way is to use the large popcorn gift tins that can be purchased at any grocery store or drug store. After the popcorn is gone, dry dog food can be stored there and easily accessed. Instead of half full bags sitting around on the floor, you'll be able to disguise this necessary (and often unsightly) staple to the pet owner's kitchen.

2. Another great idea is to prevent any mistakes from happening is to get yourself a shoe organizer for either over the door or under the bed. It will not only get your shoe collection organized and up off the floor, but it will prevent any dogs (especially puppies) from having to resist the temptation to chew.

3. Dog treats are something else that can often sit around in half empty boxes and become eyesores in an otherwise beautifully decorated space. Getting a cookie jar or small glass jar to dedicate to dog treats is a great way to get rid of the boxes and clutter. One thing to remember when going through with this step is to make sure family

members and guests know that this jar is not for human consumption!

4. Eliminating small crawl spaces in rooms can prevent from any scares and can also prevent a pet from getting trapped. Many dogs, especially puppies, can become curious and crawl into small spaces and become unable to get themselves out. If you're not around during the day, you could end up with a dog trapped behind a chair or couch with quite a mess to clean up when you get home. By eliminating these small spaces and ensuring furniture is pushed up against walls, you can avoid any potential issues.

5. If you aren't around much during the day and you have a larger dog, investing in a self refilling water bowl can be a great investment. If you have a large dog or multiple pets, this "water cooler" looking device will refill itself so you can ensure your pets aren't left high and dry while you're out.

6. If chewing has become an issue or you're worried about it becoming an issue, providing dogs with toys and bones to fulfill their natural instincts to chew can help prevent any disasters from happening. By choosing toys that don't look like normal house hold objects (stay away from toy "shoes" or even stuffed toys if you have children) so they won't be encouraged to mock the same behavior on these items in your home.

7. Limiting toys to a specific room in the house will help to prevent them from being left in various places and tripped over. Although you can't guarantee your pet

won't relocate them, storing and returning them to the same area, as well as supervising pets during play, will help prevent these often unattractive objects from being left in the middle of the living room.

8. Your backyard is an extension of your home, so making sure it's pet friendly is important. If you're going to allow your pet to access the backyard, you may want to consider a fence. Although you can use a leash, allowing your pet the freedom to run around in the back yard will be something that both you and your dog will be able to enjoy. You'll have the piece of mind knowing he or she won't run off, and your dog will be able to fully enjoy their self.

9. Just in case, investing a bottle of pet odor remover is a great idea. You'll have it in the house if you ever need it, and as pet owners know - accidents do happen. If you ever have to clean up after your pet, you'll be able to know that you won't have to deal with odor down the line.

10. Finally, pets are easy to live with if you just take the time to truly take care of them. If you're showing children how to raise a dog for the first time - giving them some of these guidelines to follow is a great way to make sure that they learn responsibility and to ensure your dog is fully cared for. By taking the time to make simple adjustments around your home for your pet, you'll be able to breathe easier and your pet will have a much happier home to live in.

Storage Solution For a Sport Equipment

Many families have children who are very interested in sports these days. They are constantly driving here, there, and everywhere to go to everyone's sports games. After a while, all of the equipment required by the sports really starts to pile up.

This sports equipment can really clutter up your home. Even if you have all of the soccer balls, lacrosse sticks, and cleats in a well-contained area, it can still look like a mess. In fact, it is not a good idea to keep these items inside because of the smell it can create.

If you've ever done the laundry after a family sports episode, you know how much dirt and grime can accumulate. Add this together with the sweat, and you have a yucky situation. Keeping everything in the house can be unsanitary to say the least.

One solution is to store everything outside. This way it's out of the way and not making a mess inside your home. There is a problem with this idea though, as rain and other outdoor elements can ruin some of the sports equipment. When you price sports equipment and clothing you know how expensive it can be. Clearly, storing things outside on their own is not a very good method.

While storing things outside on their own is not the best idea, you can store them outside in a resin shed. A resin storage shed has saved many families from the hassle and mess of having sports equipment in the home.

Resin is a very durable material that holds up well to both weather, and the things you store inside. Imagine having on place where all sport equipment goes! Cleats and bats won't be left here and there around your house anymore because everyone will know where they belong.

The smell will not contaminate your home, and the dirt will never see the inside. Containing everything in a storage shed is really a superb option. Of course, you'll want to make sure you choose the right size storage shed according to the size and amount of equipment you'll be putting into it.

Also, be sure you don't make the mistake of just letting everyone pile things in there. That only leads to mess and confusion. There are several different methods you could use for organizing the area.

One way is to put labels and bins in the shed according to the sport. So all baseball equipment would go in one area, and all soccer equipment in another. This will work well if each family member will be sharing the items and will need to find them easily.

Another option is to label and organize the area according to family member. That way, every person is responsible for his or her own area. This is a great idea if you're trying to teach individual family responsibility. It will also work if everyone is into his or her own sport and needs to keep their items separate from the others.

No matter what you decide, it is very important no to keep the dirty sports equipment inside the house. Buying a resin storage shed is a great option because it's durable and can withstand the sports items that are put in there. Make sure each family member understands the organizational system you choose so that the area is well maintained, and much less of a headache for everyone.

Finish What You Start

Find one or two proven solutions which speak to you from the list below then let your clutter be afraid, be very afraid.

1. Be Gentle On Yourself as There is Absolutely No Rush:

A home overcrowded with stuff creates foggy thinking which can prevent you from starting. Lighten your load by knowing it is not a race, there is no rush and you can't make a mistake. Just keep saying to yourself "I gently remove clutter at my own pace".

Think gently and never think of all the clutter in your entire home all at once. Only focus on one very small space at a time.

Think and feel gentle by calming and relaxing your breath. Long, slow deep breathes will oxygenate your body and relax your mind. Keep repeating "I gently remove clutter at my own pace"

2. Focus on Only One Small Space at a Time:

Start small. You are not climbing Mount Everest. Focus on one draw a week until you have finished all the draws in your home. Nothing more and nothing less.

Spend 1% of your day which is 15 minutes emptying out the contents and making brave choices about what to keep, throw out or give away. Once you have completed all the draws in the house then you can progress to shelves, under the beds and cupboards. Just focus your attention on one small space at a time. I've also provided a list below giving you links to freecycle web sites just in case you are not sure who to give your good stuff to.

. 3. Do it With a Close Friend:

Your friends are not attached to your stuff. They will have your best interest at heart and can easily talk you out of keeping too much unnecessary stuff. I know for a fact this solution has worked extremely well for many people.

4. Do it to Fabulous Music:

Find yourself the most fabulous happy uplifting piece of music that you absolutely love and play it loud. The music stops your resisting thoughts getting the better of you, uplifts your spirits and allows you to throw out more easily. Listen to some uplifting Bobby McFerrin "Don't worry be happy". I actually bought this CD and its fun to play when doing the housework or to shift the kids moods. An all time classic.

5. Find your Groove:

My groove is early in the morning when my thinking is not distributed and distracted easily. Yours might be late at night when everyone is asleep. Clear your clutter when you have the most energy and focus.

6. Sometimes its Better Just not to Involve the Kids and Other Family Members:

If I left the decisions up to my kids they would never throw out any of their old toys out. Going through my kids cupboards is much, much, much easier when they are not around. Keep in mind though it might be easier (for you personally) having them around if they are happy to give their old clothes and toys to people who will be thrilled to get them.

Thanks for reading my book.

Made in the USA
Monee, IL
06 January 2022

88174703R00095